A Sense of Belonging at Work

A sense of not belonging, that we are not accepted or valued at work can be enormously detrimental to our psychological well-being and sense of self, and can impact engagement, motivation and performance.

Based on extensive research, this accessible and practical book helps leaders understand the implications of belonging on our well-being and performance and equips them with the insight and tools to ensure their employees have a sense of belonging at work, through:

- establishing connections and developing meaningful relationships,
- identifying and leveraging values and strengths,
- developing their awareness of diversity and unconscious bias,
- fostering a psychologically safe environment in which all can speak up,
- developing an inclusive leadership mindset and
- challenging negative thinking patterns.

The strategies and tips provided will allow readers to ensure they too have a strong sense of belonging at work.

This book is designed for leaders in organisations who are responsible for the performance and well-being of their teams and for anyone who has experienced a sense of not belonging and wants to understand how to develop a sense of belonging now and in the future. It will also be of value to HR professionals and coaches, who are seeking to develop positive, inclusive workplaces.

Lee Waller is Professor of Occupational Psychology at Hult International Business School, UK, and has worked in leadership development for over seventeen years, supporting leaders to be the best of themselves at work by understanding their strengths and developing their leadership skills. Formerly Director of Research at Hult International Business School, Lee is an extensive researcher and writer in the areas of belonging, diversity and inclusion.

"Lee's insight on belonging, developed through her years of research and personal experience, provides an incredibly valuable and timely contribution. It responds to pressing questions we face regarding how we can flourish – and how we can enable others to – at work."

– **Megan Reitz,** Professor of Leadership and Dialogue, Hult International Business School / Author of *Speak Up*, *Mind Time* and *Dialogue in Organizations*

A Sense of Belonging at Work

A Guide to Improving Well-being and Performance

Lee Waller

LONDON AND NEW YORK

Cover image: Getty Images

First published 2022
by Routledge
4 Park Square, Milton Park, Abingdon, Oxon OX14 4RN

and by Routledge
605 Third Avenue, New York, NY 10158

Routledge is an imprint of the Taylor & Francis Group, an informa business

© 2022 Lee Waller

The right of Lee Waller to be identified as author of this work has been asserted in accordance with sections 77 and 78 of the Copyright, Designs and Patents Act 1988.

All rights reserved. No part of this book may be reprinted or reproduced or utilised in any form or by any electronic, mechanical, or other means, now known or hereafter invented, including photocopying and recording, or in any information storage or retrieval system, without permission in writing from the publishers.

Trademark notice: Product or corporate names may be trademarks or registered trademarks, and are used only for identification and explanation without intent to infringe.

British Library Cataloguing-in-Publication Data
A catalogue record for this book is available from the British Library

Library of Congress Cataloging-in-Publication Data
Names: Waller, Lee, author.
Title: A sense of belonging at work : a guide to improving well-being and performance / Lee Waller.
Description: Abingdon, Oxon ; New York, NY : Routledge, 2022. | Includes bibliographical references and index.
Identifiers: LCCN 2021037096 (print) | LCCN 2021037097 (ebook) | ISBN 9780367623142 (hardback) | ISBN 9780367623173 (paperback) | ISBN 9781003108849 (ebook)
Subjects: LCSH: Work—Psychological aspects. | Employees—Psychology. | Belonging (Social psychology) | Psychology, Industrial. | Organizational sociology.
Classification: LCC HF5548.8 .W2554 2022 (print) | LCC HF5548.8 (ebook) | DDC 650.1/3—dc23
LC record available at https://lccn.loc.gov/2021037096
LC ebook record available at https://lccn.loc.gov/2021037097

ISBN: 978-0-367-62314-2 (hbk)
ISBN: 978-0-367-62317-3 (pbk)
ISBN: 978-1-003-10884-9 (ebk)

DOI: 10.4324/9781003108849

Typeset in Goudy
by codeMantra

To Coral and April, with whom I always experience the warmest and most precious sense of belonging, and of home.

Contents

Acknowledgements   xi

Introduction   1
A personal experience 1
Sense of belonging at work 2
Overview of this book 3

PART 1
What it means to belong   7

1 **Belonging – a fundamental human need**   9
   Motivators of human behaviour 10
   A fundamental and universal human need 11
   The adaptive nature of belonging 15
   The neuroscience of belonging 16

2 **Factors which undermine belonging in the workplace**   22
   Quality relationships and belonging at work 23
   Adding value and belonging 26
   Difference and belonging 28
   Organisational culture 31

3 **Belonging and well-being**   36
   Belonging and our sense of self 37
      Self-efficacy, confidence and self-belief 38
      Self-esteem 39
      Coherent sense of self 42
   Mood and emotion 44

Contents

4 Belonging and performance – the trap of not belonging   48
The key to not belonging 48
Trap one: ability to be ourselves 49
    Social monitoring 49
    Conformity 50
Trap two: self-protection 52
Need for control 53
Implications for performance 57

PART 2
Establishing a sense of belonging   61

5 Developing quality relationships   63
Establishing relationships 63
Making relationships meaningful 66
    Knowing others 66
        Getting below the waterline 66
        Enquiry 68
        Presence 69
        Active listening 70
        Trust 72
    Knowing you 74
        Be you 74
        Be human 75

6 Establishing and adding our value   78
Identifying strengths 78
Leveraging strengths 83
Developing strengths 85
    Feedback 85
    Coaching 86

7 Diversity and belonging   90
The many forms of diversity 91
Evidence for the continued existence of prejudice, discrimination and bias 92
Reasons for the continuation of racial inequity 94
    Structural and systemic 94
    Unconscious bias 95
        Micro-aggressions and inequities 97
    Ignorance 98
    Fear of stepping in 100

Addressing discrimination in our workplaces 100
 Developing diverse intelligence 100
 Developing self-awareness 101
 Become an ally 102

8 Fostering psychological safety   106
What is psychological safety? 106
 What does psychological safety look like? 107
Fostering psychological safety 109
 Leader characteristics 109
 Interpersonal skills 110
 Permission to care 111
 Tolerance of failure 112
 Addressing the unspoken 113
Inclusive leadership 114

9 Being an inclusive leader   115
An inclusive mindset 116
Inclusive behaviours 117
 Collaboration 117
 Inclusive conversations 120
Courage and commitment 121

10 Reframing a sense of belonging   124
What sense of not belonging means for us 125
Unconscious cognitions 126
Challenging our inner critic 128
Step one: awareness and acceptance 130
 Curiosity and self-compassion 130
Step two: challenge 131
Step three: reframe 133

Conclusion: the journey of belonging   136

Index   139

Acknowledgements

Much of the content of this book is drawn from my doctoral research, and as such, and as always, I am grateful to the participants in that study who had the courage to share their stories with insight, honesty, and openness. I learned an enormous amount through those conversations both about belonging in the workplace and about myself. Without their accounts this book and the help that I hope it offers would not have been possible.

Thanks go to my fabulous family as well. My husband Jon and my two amazing daughters, Coral and April, all of whom have supported me in their own ways throughout the often-difficult journey of developing my thesis and the writing of this book, been tolerant of my absence and distraction, and patient with my associated stress. Thanks also go to my ever proud and supportive parents, Carol and Keith, as well as to my closest friends Laurel and Martine, who have listened to me, encouraged me and supported me continuously along the way.

Introduction

A personal experience

My first permanent full-time job was as a Marketing Assistant at a large academic publisher. I had been rescued from the Post Room (where I had been temping whilst I tried to work out what I wanted to do with my career) by one of the Marketing Managers who had spotted some semblance of potential. I worked in that role for a number of years, became promoted to Assistant Publicity Manager and then Publicity Manager. I worked hard, I got noticed, I made friends. However, I never once felt like I belonged, that I was accepted, that I fitted in. Unlike my peers, I did not have a degree, just nine GCSEs and three 'A' levels for my qualifications. And, of course, I had come up from the Post Room. That was my lack of 'fit,' my diminished value, my 'difference.'

Fast-forward ten years, past two round-the-world trips, a bachelor's degree, a master's degree, and the first of two children, and I was working as a Business Development Manager at a Business School. I now had two degrees (one more than most of my direct peers), a good insight into the business and continued to work hard. But I still did not feel that I belonged. The departmental environment was competitive and unsafe. I was continually managing my presentation, hoping not to get tripped up, caught out or mess up. I did not feel at all able to express myself, to be myself. I had no real personal connections within my team, felt unaccepted and unvalued.

Following daughter number two I got a job in Research. All my peers were incredibly bright and well qualified – many had a great deal more experience than I. But we had a shared experience of being new parents, we had a boss who valued our individual perspectives, and I worked in a role where it was incumbent on us to ask questions. I could express my concerns, admit to my absent knowledge or occasional anxieties. I could be myself, I made friends, I found my home.

DOI: 10.4324/9781003108849-1

These three occasions all had different underlying factors, but they all accumulated in the same experience – the absence or presence of a sense of belonging. Whilst I was not able to articulate it as such back then, I *was* able to talk about it. And through doing so, I discovered that many of my colleagues had experienced a sense of not belonging too, at some point in their lives. For some it was potent or enduring, for others it was faint or transient. I became increasingly aware of its manifestation in people's behaviour – I noticed withdrawal, inauthenticity, overly helpful behaviours – and I recognised them all. I started to understand that not only did a sense of not belonging impact how someone felt about themselves and their well-being, but it also had a big impact on how they behaved, and ultimately how they performed. I started to appreciate the implications of this experience not only for the individual but also for the organisation. As the next step in my academic career was to undertake a PhD, I now had my subject!

Sense of belonging at work

Through my research over the years, I have developed a nuanced understanding of the experience of belonging in the workplace. I have discovered the work of excellent scholars and practitioners who have gone before me which has elucidated the myriad connections and implications of belonging at work and resulted in the development of a model of belonging that clarifies its impact as well as what supports the development of a sense *of* belonging at work. What I have learned is that a perfect storm of factors, including a lack of being valued, a perception of difference and an absence of quality relationships can trigger a sense of not belonging. This sense in turn can undermine one's self-concept, self-esteem, self-efficacy, and a coherent sense of self. In attempting to enhance a sense of belonging and develop a positive sense of self, we often further perpetuate the experience, by acting with inauthenticity in order to 'fit in' or withdrawing or disengaging in order to 'protect' ourselves. But if we are able to take some control over the experience, if we are able to choose constructive ways to feel like we belong we can both enhance our self-concept and develop a sense of belonging, improving our well-being and our performance. This takes insight and action on our part, but also support and action on the part of our leaders and organisations.

I have discovered that there is a lot that leaders can do to encourage the development of a sense of belonging as well as support that they can offer to their teams to resolve a sense of *not* belonging. These interventions can in turn impact the well-being and performance of their teams. This understanding is what has led to the publication of this book. A book designed to help leaders understand the implications of belonging on our well-being and performance, what they can do to foster a sense of belonging for their teams, as well as what they can do themselves, to ensure that they feel like they belong in their workplace. If this sounds of value to you, then please read on.

Overview of this book

This book is divided into two parts: **Part 1: What it means to belong** explores what contributes to a sense of belonging in the workplace, and the impact it has on our thoughts, feelings and behaviour. These first four chapters provide insight into the significance of belonging to our experience at work, our well-being and performance, offering both an opportunity for personal reflection and an understanding of the contextual and behavioural signals that might indicate that a member of our team is experiencing a sense of not belonging.

Chapter 1: Belonging – a fundamental human need presents the plentiful research that demonstrates that our need to belong is a fundamental human need, motivating a wealth of behaviour with implications for our well-being and performance in the workplace. As a constituent of all the grand theories of motivation, a driver of our tendency to form into groups, as well as playing a role in many of the sociological and psychological phenomena in ancient as well as modern societies, belonging is also able to direct what we think and what we feel. This chapter closes with consideration of the neurological evidence that suggests that belonging is in fact an adaptive driver, vital to our very existence as a species.

Chapter 2: Factors which undermine belonging in the workplace introduces the factors, situations and environments that can undermine our sense of belonging in the workplace: an absence of quality relationships; a sense of not adding value; and believing oneself to be different from those with whom we work. It discusses too, the organisational cultures in which a sense of not belonging can manifest. This chapter draws on the accounts from my research (whilst changing names), to illuminate the individual lived experience. My hope is that should your experience resonate with those accounts that this and the following chapters may help to validate and normalise that experience, as well as provide you with an understanding of the factors which may put your team at risk of not belonging and undermine their well-being and performance.

Chapter 3: Belonging and well-being introduces the core factor implicated in the influence of a sense of not belonging on our well-being – the impact that this has on our self-concept. This chapter describes how our sense of self is informed by both who we are in relation to others and what we believe others think about us – and thus, how feeling that we do not belong and are not accepted can undermine our self-concept. Drawing again on the accounts of those interviewed, this chapter illustrates the impact of a sense of not belonging on our self-efficacy, our self-esteem and our sense of a consistent self-concept. It illuminates too the emotional impact of a sense of not belonging and how our interpretation of both the experience and our emotional response to it can galvanise the negative impact of a sense of not belonging on our psychological well-being.

Chapter 4: Belonging and performance – the trap of not belonging explores the impact of a sense of not belonging on our thoughts and behaviour and ultimately on our performance at work, undermining our capacity to contribute, add value and reach our potential. It discusses too, two traps into which we often fall when we feel we do not belong: The first being our tendency to conform, defer, behave inauthentically in an attempt to fit in; and the second our efforts to protect ourselves by withdrawing, detaching and disengaging, undermining our ability to connect, add value and as such, to belong. This chapter also emphasises the role that our sense of control and ability to enhance our belonging plays in determining whether we will respond constructively or detrimentally to feeling we do not belong at work.

Part 2: Establishing a sense of belonging turns attention to the implications of belonging for organisations and for leaders, and offers practical insights and guidance as to how we can support the development of a sense of belonging for our teams, as well as for ourselves. It begins with **Chapter 5: Developing quality relationships**, which discusses the means through which we can create opportunities to connect with others, such as through collaboration, mentoring and out of work activities. It explores too, how we can ensure that the relationships we develop are meaningful and offers insight as to how to build human connections, and the importance of modelling, as I hope I do in sharing my own experiences, the courage to be open and to be all of ourselves at work.

Chapter 6: Establishing and adding our value offers further insight to help our teams as well as ourselves, to identify and leverage their strengths in the workplace, supporting both their sense of adding value and belonging and also maximising their performance. It discusses the importance of autonomy and control to encourage constructive responses to a sense of not belonging by seeking out opportunities to add value, to develop relationships and to identify connections. This chapter also introduces two simple models for supporting the development of the skills of our teams, through providing regular, constructive feedback and a solutions-focused approach to coaching.

Chapter 7: Diversity and belonging offers an opportunity to enhance awareness of both the continued discrimination and bias present in our workplaces, as well as the steps we can take to address these biases and improve racial equity. It begins with consideration of the many forms of bias and how they play out in the workplace, the evidence for the continued racial discrimination in our organisations and the potential reasons for its endurance. This chapter moves on to explore how we can move ourselves along the path of inclusion through enhancing our awareness of both the lived experience of those from diverse groups, develop awareness of our own potential biases and cultivate the confidence to step in as an ally to those from diverse groups.

Chapter 8: Fostering psychological safety explores the critical construct of psychological safety and the role it plays in supporting our teams' ability to speak up, offer ideas and contributions, and as such add value and establish a sense of belonging at work. It discusses what psychological safety is and looks like, and how to recognise the presence or absence of psychological safety in our teams, including a simple assessment tool. This chapter goes on to explore how we can foster psychological safety by acting with authenticity, humility, vulnerability and compassion, by being tolerant of failure and addressing the unspoken challenges in our teams.

Chapter 9: Being an inclusive leader explores the importance of inclusive leadership to developing a sense of belonging at work, to speaking up and offering contributions and to addressing bias and discrimination in the workplace. This chapter discusses three key elements of inclusive leadership: An inclusive mindset of curiosity, openness, compassion and respect; inclusive behaviours of collaboration and integration and the courage and commitment to share power, trust our teams, challenge ourselves and others and stay true to our values of equity and inclusion.

The final chapter, **Chapter 10: Reframing a sense of belonging**, turns attention to the meaning that we place on our experience of not belonging in terms of what it says about who we are. It discusses our tendency to attribute the cause of our sense of not belonging to ourselves, the negative automatic thoughts this can trigger, and the disarming self-directed emotions that can be induced. This chapter lays out a three-step process designed to tackle these thoughts: Awareness of how and when these thoughts arise; challenge of the assumptions and evidence on which they are based; and reframing of those thoughts as alternative, positive beliefs. It closes with a simple tool for capturing this process and challenging our negative thoughts and inner critic ultimately enhancing our psychological well-being.

Part 1
What it means to belong

1
Belonging – a fundamental human need

> Belonging is about feeling as if you have a place, as if you matter as if you have a set of relationships that really matter with people.
>
> – Neil, Head of Residential Care Home

Belonging matters. Type 'sense of belonging' into Google and you will come across 148 million hits.[1] Make your way through the first part of this book, and you will discover the plethora of research that has been dedicated to uncovering the causes, consequences and power of this phenomenon. Talk about 'belonging' with anyone from an eight-year-old child to a 90-year-old grandmother, a stay-at-home mum, a bin-man, an accountant, a CEO or a neuro-surgeon – they will all know what it is that you mean. And most of them will spontaneously, if privately, recall a time when they either felt like they did belong, or a time when they felt they did not.

During my lifetime I have been a part of two close-knit social groups. The first, a group of slightly mis-fitting goths, hippies and rockers, in my late teens. The second a group of bright, passionate, articulate house-music lovers in my mid-twenties. During both of these times, these groups kept me grounded, solid, safe and self-assured. They were my tribe, my support and they affirmed my sense of self. I see similar groups all around me all the time – in pubs, restaurants, on beaches, in the workplace – groups of people who click, connect, understand and support each other. And they make me smile with vicarious pleasure. The impact of belonging to these groups on our well-being, our ability to be ourselves, to feel good about ourselves, is tangible – visceral and significant.

I have already referred to my experiences of the opposite in the introduction to this book, and sadly this is an equally prevalent and powerful experience for others: The classic scenario depicted in so many teen programmes, of being

DOI: 10.4324/9781003108849-3

the last to be picked for the football team; the experience of the lonely school bench or empty chairs in the work canteen; not being invited to the party or the meeting; being excluded from the private joke or simply an unprovoked sense that you just do not fit. With these experiences comes the urge to withdraw, to self-protect, to 'pretend' and to not be ourselves. Perhaps this is a rite of passage to adulthood. But the emotional and psychological impact is still acute, it is often painful and as we mature, it can become troubling and the impact enduring.

So, why is the experience, whether positive or negative, so very powerful? Why is it felt so acutely? Why is it able to affect both how we think, feel and behave? Put simply, the answer is because human beings are social animals. Belonging keeps us safe and keeps us alive.

Motivators of human behaviour

Psychology is the science of behaviour, and for the past couple of centuries it has been incumbent upon psychologists to determine why we behave the way that we do. What is it that directs our thinking and motivates our behaviour? This work has resulted in, amongst many, many other things, the development of a number of theories of motivation.[2,3]

Abraham Maslow's *Hierarchy of Needs*, whilst not always finding scholarly support, is nevertheless the most familiar theory of human motivation, and one which has made its way into common parlance.[4] According to the theory, our behaviour is driven by a desire to satisfy one of five basic human needs: Physiological needs; safety needs; belongingness or love needs; self-esteem needs; and self-actualisation needs (see Figure 1.1). Maslow proposed that these needs are related to each other in a hierarchy insofar as the higher needs will not receive attention until the lower needs are at least partially satisfied, and that behaviour will be focused primarily on the satisfaction of that need until it is.

Whilst this argument is somewhat common-sensical – if I am homeless and hungry, I am unlikely to be distracted by a need to be creative – it might not necessarily be the case that a sense of connection or a perception of respect from others would be of no importance in that scenario. And indeed, whilst the needs outlined do resonate with other theories, research has found little support for their hierarchical nature.[5] However, Maslow's *Hierarchy of Needs* does help us to understand how our behaviour becomes directed by our most immediate and pressing need, one of which, according to Maslow, is the need to belong.

The need to belong is also a component of Alderfer's three-stage model, including *existence*, *relatedness* and *growth* needs (ERG).[6] Existence needs refer to the concern with subsistence such as food, water, money and working conditions;

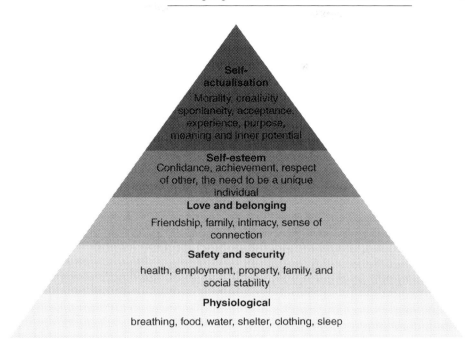

Figure 1.1 Maslow's *Hierarchy of Needs*, 1943.[7]

relatedness refers to our need to develop and maintain interpersonal relationships with friends, family, peers and other working groups; and growth refers to our need for personal development, such as our ability to contribute, and to be creative. McClelland's *3-Needs Theory*[8] also identified three motivational needs in which achievement referred to the need to excel and succeed, power referred to the need to influence others and affiliation referred to the need to be liked and approved of. Finally, Deci and Ryan's *Self-Determination Theory*[9] suggests that human motivation is determined by the pursuit of the three innate needs of autonomy, competence and again, relatedness.

As such, whilst there is a lack of agreement in terms of the number and types of need that drive human behaviour, there are clear and apparent parallels across the theories, and all of the models consider the need to belong, described as 'belongingness,' 'relatedness' or 'affiliation,' as a fundamental motivator of the way that we behave.

A fundamental and universal human need

This need to belong is central to the work of notable social psychologists Roy Baumeister and Mark Leary, who developed the *Belonging Hypothesis*.[10]

According to their theory *"Human beings are fundamentally and pervasively motivated by a need to belong, that is, by a strong desire to form and maintain enduring interpersonal attachments."*[11] The need to belong, they argue, has a significant impact on how we think, feel and behave, and drives behaviour designed to enhance our sense of belonging. As you will discover in the chapters in the first part of this book, there is a wealth of research that supports the significant impact of the need to belong, or the impact of thwarting of the need to belong on our well-being and behaviour. But the fundamental nature of the need also finds theoretical and scientific support from a number of disciplines. Anthropological studies, for example, consistently found that people in all societies will naturally form into groups. And sociological studies, particularly those exploring in-group behaviour have found that individuals will spontaneously form into groups, develop in-group social bonds and treat members of their own group with favouritism compared to members of other groups.[12, 13, 14]

In the classic Robbers Cave experiments, Muzafer Sherif and his colleagues randomly allocated 12-year-old boys into two groups in order to explore the development of social bonds and the concept of ethnocentrism – that we are driven to preferably evaluate aspects of our own group.[15, 16] Keeping the two groups apart for the first week whilst they worked to achieve common goals (such as completing a treasure hunt or building apparatus), the authors first found that the two groups rapidly formed bonds between members of their group. They developed a group structure by instituting a hierarchy of status positions, established group norms and attitudes, such as naming their groups and referring to objects as 'ours,' and created group characteristics, such as being 'tough.' The authors also found that when competition was introduced between the two groups, fierce opposition developed, expressed through actions such as burning the other group's flag or eating their food, as well as characterising them in unfavourable terms.

Whilst it could be that development of these intra-group bonds was a necessary requirement of working effectively together in order to successfully achieve group goals, *Social Identity Theory* researchers have found that even when no requirement to work together exists, arbitrary assignment to groups results in in-group favouritism. For example, over a series of studies, John Howard and Myron Rothbart[17] found that arbitrary assignment to groups resulted in individuals allocating more favourable statements (such as 'I took disadvantaged kids on a 2-week vacation') to members of their in-group and describing them with more favourable adjectives (such as friendly, likable or cooperative). They also more accurately recognised unfavourable behaviours associated with the members of the out-group than they did their own group. These types of studies all suggest that the need to belong is so fundamental to us as human beings that it not only drives our behaviour but can also direct our *thinking*.

Evidence of the universal nature of the need to belong and the cognitive and behavioural impact of this need is found all around us, in all modern societies, in many modern sociological phenomena. For example, in cities all around the world, adolescents, young adults and now increasingly children are joining gangs. Recent UK government statistics put the number of children in gangs between the age of 10 and 15 at 27,000, and 6% of 10–19-year-olds report belonging to a gang.[18] Whilst there are many socio-economic factors related to gang membership, many members are motivated to join gangs for the sense of identity and sense of belonging they afford.[19] We see this too in the formation of school and workplace cliques – exclusive circles of individuals who spend time together and make it clear that not anyone can join their group, either actively or passively excluding and ostracising others.[20] These cliques form primarily through a desire to establish an identity, a sense of acceptance and belonging.

As these two examples indicate, our need to belong can often evolve into negative, destructive and prejudiced attitudes and actions. Racism, xenophobia and homophobia are all examples of our inherent need to think better about ourselves by thinking badly about and acting poorly towards others. These patterns of thought can be so engrained and fundamental that they become blind to logic, reason or rational argument. But they serve our need to belong. Steve Taylor, senior lecturer in psychology at Leeds Beckett University, argues that these forms of prejudice are a self-defence mechanism designed to protect us from feelings of insignificance and inadequacy.[21] He proposes that racism involves five different stages of defence, the first of which is driven by a need to belong – a desire to establish an identity by affiliating with and establishing a sense of belonging to a group. However, in attempting to strengthen this sense of identity and belonging, this at first innocuous motivation can move to enmity, hostility and conflict with 'other' groups. Empathy towards the 'other' diminishes as compassion and benevolence towards the in-group increases. The 'other' becomes homogenised, prejudice generalised and the 'other' eventually demonised – all, in part, in service of our need to belong.

We see it too in other well-established and common phenomena: *Groupthink*, for example. Groupthink describes the group decision-making process whereby the drive to maintain unity overrides the drive to employ rational and objective decision-making processes, resulting in poor, and sometimes catastrophic decisions.[22] Groupthink typically occurs under pressured and stressful circumstances, and in groups which are close-knit and cohesive, and ideologically homogenous, that is they share the same beliefs and ideologies. This ideological homogeneity satisfies the need to belong and supports a sense of self-esteem and well-being,[23] and as such thinking is directed to support rather than disrupt belonging, through at times irrational agreement.

One of the most notorious examples of groupthink is the Space Shuttle Challenger disaster of 1986, where millions around the world watched on live television as the spacecraft exploded minutes after take-off. The ultimate cause of the disaster was the failure of an O-ring, a component of the rocket booster. NASA had been warned by the contractor responsible for the component's development the day before the launch, that the unprecedented cold weather may affect the O-ring's performance. However, on the day of the launch, under pressure from NASA to avoid further delays, the contractor's engineers held a private meeting, and within five minutes conformed to the will of NASA and agreed to launch without further objection. The desire to maintain unity ultimately led to the death of all seven members of crew.

Bystander apathy, or the bystander effect, is another commonly observed phenomenon also in part motivated by our need to belong. The bystander effect is a well evidenced social scenario whereby the larger the group of onlookers the less likely it is for someone to come to the aid of a person in need.[24] The effect was first explored following the murder of Kitty Genovese outside her apartment building in New York, on 13 March 1964. Kitty was stabbed on two separate occasions during her attack which occurred over a time span of half an hour. Her screams were overheard by 38 neighbours, none of whom came to help.

The attack sparked a surge of interest as to why nobody offered assistance, and a number of studies followed. Most of these studies induced participants into believing that someone was in need of help, for example, believing they were struggling to open a filing cabinet or even having a seizure.[25, 26] The potential influence of the need to belong on the bystander effect was identified in Bibb Latane and John Darley's later research which concluded that one possible reason for the lack of helping behaviour was participant's concern about committing a social blunder or not being seen to adhere to social norms.[27]

Their study involved participants believing that they had seen the experimenter receiving an electric shock and explored under what conditions the participants were more or least likely to step in to help. The experiment involved five conditions: The participant observed the event alone; they knew another participant also observed the event but could not see them or be seen; they could see the response of the other participant, but they could not be seen themselves; the participant could be seen by the bystander but not vice versa; and finally, the participant could see the bystander's response *and* could be seen by the bystander. The researchers found that the greater the level of communication the more the helping decreased, with those participants who could see and be seen helping the least. The authors concluded that these results suggest that the passivity of the bystander when the participant could see them

Belonging – a fundamental human need

indicated social norms – expected ways of behaving – and therefore helped to guide behaviour. In addition, a concern about committing a social blunder (by helping when it did not appear that helping was expected) was also involved for the participants whose response could be seen by the bystander. As such, the behaviour observed in the bystander effect is driven in part by a need to belong and concerns with replicating social norms and not engaging in behaviour which may lead to punishment through social exclusion.

It seems therefore that the need to belong does matter, and is a fundamental motivator of much of our thinking and our behaviour and is implicated in many well-established psychological phenomena.

But why is it that we have such a fundamental need to be part of a group?

The adaptive nature of belonging

Evolutionary theorists would argue that this need to belong has an important adaptive function. Evolutionary psychology aims to understand how our evolutionary history contributes to the development of patterns of thought and behaviour that support our reproduction and survival.[28] Essentially, the argument holds that many of the ways that we think and behave now are a legacy of thoughts and behaviours that supported our survival as we evolved as a species.

Consider that tens of thousands of years ago, early humans were ill-equipped to survive. We were not speedy, we were not particularly strong, we were not ferocious and we were not able to escape capture through taking flight or burrowing underground. What assured our survival was the development of universal patterns of behaviour, including cooperation beyond close kin and establishing social norms.[29] These facilitated the development of social groups which offered protection, nurture and support.[30] Back on the African savannah and then the plains and forests of Europe, behaving in cooperative and harmonious ways would have resulted in group inclusion, whereas those who engaged in less cooperative behaviours would be more likely to be excluded and thus less likely to survive.[31, 32] According to evolutionary theorists therefore, the need to belong would have supported our survival by encouraging us to behave in ways which would enhance our likelihood of being accepted and included in groups and less likely to starve to death or be eaten by a hungry lion.

This more primal survival nature of the need to belong is evident in modern behaviours and in modern societies, such as the development of the workplace cliques and gangs considered earlier. As well as being motivated to feel accepted and included, children, adolescents and adults are motivated to join exclusive cliques and neighbourhood gangs also because of the safety and protection they afford, from both other members of those groups and from the members of others.[33]

The neuroscience of belonging

One of the strongest indicators that any form of human behaviour is adaptive is whether or not it has an underlying physiological component. One of the most commonly known physiological survival systems is our *fight-flight-freeze* response – our physiological response to threat. During these occurrences, our brain, specifically our amygdala which is responsible for processing emotion such as perceiving fear, identifies the threat and sends a signal to another part of our brain, the hypothalamus. This is responsible for physiological and hormonal regulation and activates our sympathetic nervous system. Our heart rate increases sending blood and oxygen to our peripheral muscles, principally the arms and legs, preparing us to fight or to run.[34]

These physiological changes are responsible for the flushing of our faces, pounding of our hearts, dryness of our mouths and catching of our throats when we encounter an anxiety provoking situation, such as an important interview, a keynote speech or a first date. Sadly, as blood and oxygen are being sent to our muscles and away from our brains, they are also responsible for the enormous drop off in our cognitive capacity during those moments. These are those times when we find ourselves struggling to speak or remember our own name let alone articulate an intelligent response to a complex question.[35]

As such, what drives us to act under threat and pressure now is the same innate need that drove us thousands of years ago – survival. In our typically sophisticated and modern world what our brains are responding to, what it is that we must 'survive' has clearly changed beyond scope: We are now more concerned with losing our jobs, our reputations, our homes or our suitors, than losing our lives. However, when under threat, our neurological and physiological responses are precisely the same as those of our distant ancestors.

Whilst much less salient and dramatic, our response to both a sense of belonging and our response to a *threat* to our belonging also have neurological underpinnings which indicate that the need to belong may also be adaptive and critical to our survival. The first is how we *feel* when we belong. If we consider those times of acceptance – being part of a solid friendship group, being asked to join in, feeling accepted, validated and valued. It feels good. It is a pleasurable feeling that we crave and of which we want more. Recent research has found that the experience of belonging actually stimulates dopamine – the feel-good hormone which is involved in reward and reinforcement and motivates us to do more of what feels good. This is a potent reward-motivation hormone which is responsible for directing much of our reward-motivated behaviour.[36] It is the same chemical that is released when we eat chocolate, have sex, take addictive recreational drugs such as cocaine, or play videogames.[37, 38] The release of this hormone during bonding and positive social interaction makes these experiences similarly rewarding and inherently pleasurable, encouraging us to seek out social interaction and encouraging the belongingness motivation.[39]

Social bonding has also been found to be related to another hormone, oxytocin.[40] This hormone is critical to reproduction, stimulating contraction of the uterus during childbirth and the movement of milk to the breast following stimulation, and is also involved in sexual activity including penile erection and orgasm, as well as mother-child bonding, behaviour which ensures our children's survival.[41] As such, oxytocin is clearly vitally important to our survival as a species. Interestingly, research has also found that injection of oxytocin promotes pro-social behaviour, empathy, trust and helping, all behaviours which promote inclusion and belonging.[42, 43] Given the importance of this hormone to our reproduction and survival as a species, its role in the social behaviour of humans suggests again that belonging is also vital to our survival.

Perhaps the most striking connection between belonging and the make-up of our brains is the pain we experience when we feel that we do *not* belong. Being purposefully excluded from the workplace clique, being rejected by a lover or a friend, being ignored at a party or left out of the chat in a meeting, hurts. For those of us unlucky enough to have experienced this, and let us be frank, that is most likely all of us at some time or another – we know that it is painful, and that pain can feel physical. When I teach and talk about the sense of not belonging, I always, involuntarily clasp my hands to my stomach – the experience is so physical, represented by a tight knot that makes me flinch.

The reason for this acute experience has been illuminated by our colleagues in the field of neuroscience. They have uncovered that social pain – the pain experienced through interpersonal rejection, may feel acutely painful because it actually activates the same parts of the brain as physical pain. This part of the brain is called the anterior cingulate cortex (ACC), and it is known to be activated by physical pain, particularly the affective rather than sensory part.[44] That is to say, how we emotionally and psychologically respond to pain. In studies that manipulate the experience of inclusion or exclusion (by being excluded or included in a virtual game of ball toss) the ACC of those who were excluded was found to be activated more than those who were included.[45] The research also found that those who were excluded in the game had more activation of the right ventral prefrontal cortex (RVPFC) but that the greater the self-reported distress the lower the activation of the RVPFC. This part of the brain is involved in the reduction of physical pain symptoms,[46] and it would seem to play a regulatory role in diminishing the distress of social exclusion.

This neuroscientific evidence offers some substantial support to the argument that the need to belong is a fundamental and adaptive human need, so vital to our existence that as humans became more dependent on each other for survival, our brains evolved to adopt the same neural pathways involved in physical pain for social pain in order to alert us to a threat to our social inclusion and ultimately our survival.

This is likely why so many of us have experienced both the warm pleasure of belonging and the cold pain of not belonging. And it is also why, as the following chapters will explore further, not belonging has such a significant impact on how we feel, how we think and how we behave. It is, therefore, worthy of exploring, and, in particular, worthy of understanding how we can ensure that we and others have a sense of belonging, in all areas of our lives, not least of which the workplace, to support both our well-being and our performance. We will start this exploration by considering what it is that contributes to us feeling that we do not belong at work.

Notes

1 As of September 2021.
2 Borkowski, N. (2005). Content theories of motivation. In N. Borkowski & N. Borkowski (Eds.) Boston, MA: Jones and Bartlett Publishers, 113–138. http://doi.org/10.1007/978-3-030-02470-3_83-1
3 Baumeister, R. F., & Leary, M. R. (1995). The need to belong: Desire for interpersonal attachments as a fundamental human motivation. *Psychological Bulletin*, 117(3), 497–529. http://doi:10.1037//0033-2909.117.3.497
4 Maslow, A. H. (1943). A theory of human motivation. *Psychological Review*, 50(4), 370–396. http://doi:10.1037/h0054346
5 Wahba, M. A., & Bridwell, L. G. (1976). Maslow reconsidered: A review of research on the need hierarchy theory. *Organizational Behavior and Human Performance*, 15(2), 212–240. http://doi.org/10.1016/0030-5073(76)90038-6
6 Alderfer, C. P. (1972). *Existence, relatedness, and growth: Human needs in organizational settings*. New York: Free Press.
7 Maslow, A. H. (1943). A theory of human motivation. *Psychological Review*, 50(4), 370–396. http://doi:10.1037/h0054346
8 McClelland, D. C. (1985). *Human motivation*. Glenview, IL: Scott, Foreman.
9 Deci, E. L., & Ryan, R. M. (2000). The what and why of goal pursuits: Human needs and the self-determination of behaviour. *Psychological Inquiry*, 11, 227–268. http://doi:10.1207/s15327965pli1104_01

10 Baumeister, R. F., & Leary, M. R. (1995). The need to belong: Desire for interpersonal attachments as a fundamental human motivation. *Psychological Bulletin*, 117(3), 497–529. http://doi:10.1037//0033-2909.117.3.497

11 Baumeister, R. F., & Leary, M. R. (1995). The need to belong: Desire for interpersonal attachments as a fundamental human motivation. *Psychological Bulletin*, 117(3), 497–529. http://doi:10.1037//0033-2909.117.3.497

12 Sherif, C. W., Harvey, O. J., White, B. J., Hood, W. R., & Sherif, C. W. (1961). *Intergroup conflict and cooperation: The Robbers Cave experiment* (Vol. 10). Norman: University of Oklahoma Press.

13 Sherif, M., Harvey, O. J., White, B. J., Hood, W. R., & Sherif, C. W. (1988). *The robbers cave experiment: Intergroup conflict and cooperation*. Middletown, CT: Wesleyan University Press.

14 Tajfel, H., Billig, M. G., Bundy, R. P., & Flament, C. (1971). Social categorization and intergroup behaviour. *European Journal of Social Psychology*, 1, 149–178. http://doi:10.1002/ejsp.2420010202

15 Sherif, C. W., Harvey, O. J., White, B. J., Hood, W. R., & Sherif, C. W. (1961). *Intergroup conflict and cooperation: The Robbers Cave experiment* (Vol. 10). Norman: University of Oklahoma Press.

16 Brewer, M. B., & Campbell, D. T. (1976). *Ethnocentrism and intergroup attitudes: East African evidence*. New York: Halstead.

17 Howard, J. W., & Rothbart, M. (1980). Social categorization and memory for in-group and out-group behavior. *Journal of Personality and Social Psychology*, 38(2), 301. http://doi.org/10.1037/0022-3514.38.2.301

18 Centre for Social Justice. (2009). *Dying to belong: An in-depth review of street gangs in Britain*. London: Centre for Social Justice.

19 Baccaglini, W. F. (1993). *Project youth gang-drug prevention: A state-wide research study*. Rensselaer: New York State Division for Youth.

20 Sias, P. (2009). Social ostracism, cliques, and outcasts. In Lutgen-Sandvik, P. & Sypher, B. D. (eds) *Destructive organizational communication: Processes, consequences, and constructive ways of organizing*. Abingdon: Routledge, 145–163.

21 Taylor, S. (2018). The Psychology of racism: Racism is a sign of a lack of psychological maturity and integration. *Psychology Today*. https://www.psychologytoday.com/gb/blog/out-the-darkness/201801/the-psychology-racism

22 Janis, I. L. (1972). *Victims of groupthink: A psychological study of foreign policy decisions and fiascos*. Boston, MA: Houghton Mifflin.

23 Motyl, M., Iyer, R., Oishi, S., Trawalter, S., & Nosek, B. A. (2014). How ideological migration geographically segregates groups. *Journal of Experimental Social Psychology*, 51, 1–14. http://doi.org/10.31234/osf.io/25myb

24 Darley, J. M., & Latané, B. (1968). Bystander intervention in emergencies: Diffusion of responsibility. *Journal of Personality and Social Psychology*, 8(4p1), 377. http://doi.org/10.1037/h0025589

25 Darley, J. M., & Latané, B. (1968). Bystander intervention in emergencies: Diffusion of responsibility. *Journal of Personality and Social Psychology*, 8(4p1), 377. http://doi.org/10.1037/h0025589

26 Latané, B., & Rodin, J. (1969). A lady in distress: Inhibiting effects of friends and strangers on bystander intervention. *Journal of Experimental Social Psychology*, 5(2), 189–202. http://doi.org/10.1016/0022-1031(69)90046-8

27 Latané, B., & Darley, J. M. (1976). *Help in a crisis: Bystander response to an emergency*. New York: General Learning Press.

28 Leger, D. W. (1991). *Biological foundations of behaviour*. New York: Harper Collins.

29 Hill, K., Barton, M., & Hurtado, A. M. (2009). The emergence of human uniqueness: Characters underlying behavioral modernity. *Evolutionary Anthropology: Issues, News, and Reviews*, 18(5), 187–200. http://doi.org/10.1002/evan.20224

30 Coon, C. S. (1946). The universality of natural groupings in human societies. *The Journal of Educational Sociology*, 20(3), 163–168. http://doi.org/10.2307/2263780

31 Caporael, L. R. (1997). The evolution of truly social cognition: The core configurations model. *Personality and Social Psychology Review*, 1(4), 276–298. http://doi.org/10.1207/s15327957pspr0104_1

32 Leakey, R. E., & Lewin, R. (1992). *Origins reconsidered: In search of what makes us human*. New York: Doubleday.

33 Baccaglini, W. F. (1993). *Project youth gang-drug prevention: A state-wide research study*. Rensselaer: New York State Division for Youth.

34 Blascovich, J., & Tomaka, J. (1996). The biopsychosocial model of arousal regulation. In M. P. Zanna (Ed.) *Advances in experimental social psychology*, vol. 28. San Diego, CA: Academic Press, 1–51. http://doi.org/10.1016/S0065-2601(08)60235-X

35 Frankenhaeuser, M. (1986). A psychobiological framework for research on humans' stress and coping. In M. H. Appley, and R. Trumbull (Eds.) *Dynamics of stress: Physiological, psychological, and social perspectives*. New York: Plenum, 101–116.

36 Berridge, K. C., Robinson, T. E., & Aldridge, J. W. (February 2009). Dissecting components of reward: 'Liking,' 'wanting,' and learning. *Current Opinion in Pharmacology*, 9(1), 65–73. http://doi:10.1016/j.coph.2008.12.014.

37 Arias-Carrión, O., & Pöppel, E. (2007). Dopamine, learning and reward-seeking behavior. *Acta Neurobiologiae Experimentalis*, 67(4), 481–488.

38 Wise, R. A. (1996). Addictive drugs and brain stimulation reward. *Annual Review of Neuroscience*, 19, 319–340.

39 Carter, C. S. (1998). Neuroendocrine perspectives on social attachment and love. *Psychoneuroendocrinology*, 23(8), 779–818. http://doi.org/10.1016/S0306-4530(98)00055-9

40 Gangestad, S. W., & Grebe, N. M. (2017). Hormonal systems, human social bonding, and affiliation. *Hormones and Behavior*, 91, 122–135. http://doi.org/10.1016/j.yhbeh.2016.08.005

41 Magon, N., & Kalra, S. (2011). The orgasmic history of oxytocin: Love, lust, and labor. *Indian Journal of Endocrinology and Metabolism*, 15(Suppl3), S156–S161. https://doi.org/10.4103/2230-8210.84851

42 Putnam, P. T., Roman, J. M., Zimmerman, P. E., & Gothard, K. M. (2016). Oxytocin enhances gaze-following responses to videos of natural social behavior in adult male rhesus monkeys. *Psychoneuroendocrinology*, 72, 47–53.

43 McQuaid, R. J., McInnis, O. A., Abizaid, A., & Anisman, H. (2014). Making room for oxytocin in understanding depression. *Neuroscience & Biobehavioral Reviews*, 45, 305–322.

44 Rainville, P., Duncan, G. H., Price, D. D., Carrier, B., & Bushnell, M. C. (1997). Pain affect encoded in human anterior cingulate but not somatosensory cortex. *Science*, 277(5328), 968–971.
45 Eisenberger, N. I., Lieberman, M. D., & Williams, K. D. (2003). Does rejection hurt? An fMRI study of social exclusion. *Science*, 302(5643), 290–292.
46 Petrovic, P., & Ingvar, M. (2002). Imaging cognitive modulation of pain processing. *Pain*, 95(1), 1–5.

2
Factors which undermine belonging in the workplace

> It comes back to the key to of all of this. I think it's feeling valued, but at the same time feeling you've got a place in the organisation, whether it's a purpose or, it's an acceptance isn't it I suppose.
>
> – Stuart, Foreign and Commonwealth Office

Whilst a sense of belonging to our families and social groups is vital to us as human beings, having a sense of belonging in the workplace has also become increasingly important. Our offices, factories, warehouses, schools, hospitals and other venues and institutions of employment are where we spend the majority of our day. With work becoming ever more significant in modern life, it now provides us with much of the social support that used to be gained primarily from extended families and community,[1] and it is therefore fertile ground for a sense of not belonging to take root. In my work with leaders, I have found that as many as 72% have experienced a sense of not belonging at work (16% had not, and 12% were not sure). Because for so many of us, our work is central to who we are and affords us a sense of self-worth and validation, feeling that we do not belong in the workplace can have a significant impact on our well-being and our very sense of who we are.

However, as my research has found, perhaps your experience reflects, and the following chapter will demonstrate, whilst still a key factor, belonging at work involves more than just affiliation, relationships, social connection – it also involves a sense of commonality and, perhaps critically, a sense that we are valued and are making a valuable contribution to our teams and our place of work. Without one or all of these things, work can be experienced as a very lonely environment.

Research has identified three key factors that can trigger someone to feel like they do *not* belong at work: An absence of quality relationships; a sense of not being valued; and a lack of commonality or shared characteristics with those with whom we work.[2] For the sake of simplicity and clarity I am separating these out in this chapter. But as you will see from the following pages, there is a great deal of cross-over between these factors. Typically, one of these elements will not necessarily result in a significant sense of not belonging. Not having quality relationships, for example, may leave us feeling outside of 'the group' but not necessarily result in a sense of not belonging; not feeling valued at work may result in us feeling demotivated and disengaged, but not necessarily like we are an outsider; and being part of a minority demographic may make us feel 'different,' but may not leave us feeling like we do not belong. But what we tend to find in our lived experience as well as in the research is that a sense of not belonging often involves a complex interwoven web of one or two of these factors, and at times a perfect storm of all three. What is often critical to the impact of these factors is the organisational environment in which they occur – whilst not directly *causing* a sense of not belonging, it can provide the context in which a sense of not belonging can both manifest and be maintained.

Quality relationships and belonging at work

Relationships at work do matter to belonging. It is as important to us to have a sense of connection and affiliation in the workplace as it is outside of it. But for these relationships to be significant to our sense of belonging they need to be meaningful. Most of us have any number of relationships at work – whether they are with our boss, members of our teams or connections and networks beyond those boundaries. But knowing someone well enough to say, 'good morning,' to catch up on the weekend's events or to discuss the requirements of an important project does not qualify as a quality relationship. Research has found that meaningful association, feeling understood and appreciated, supported and accepted are most important for a sense of relatedness and belonging.[3, 4] As such, for a workplace relationship to support our sense of affiliation and belonging it needs to offer opportunities for interactions which are characterised by empathy, trust and understanding.[5, 6] These relationships help us to feel cared for, understood, validated and valued by the other.[7]

An absence of these relationships takes many forms. One of the interviewees in my doctoral research had started a new job in business development. As someone who was very sociable, used to establishing relationships with clients and to making connections, building relationships at work had never been a challenge. But in her new organisation things were different. As a small company, if you were not part of the leadership 'clique' you were essentially an outsider, and as much as she tried to find her way in, the doors were always closed. She told me:

> You were definitely part of the leading gang or you weren't. And part of the leading gang meant that you were strong on banter, that you went out and socialised, got absolutely pissed as a fart with everybody, and you went along with the general consensus. So, there was little space for somebody who was not brazen and forthright and extravert and of that bantery laddish type of persuasion.

Without colleagues that she could be close enough to, to share her concerns, Delia made the assumption that everyone else thought it was fine.

> I just assumed that everybody else was far more resilient than I was, and you know, they were just dealing with it better, and that they were more somehow, more whole human beings because they were able to embrace it and you know, have such a laugh doing it and have such fun and everything. 'Why can't I handle this? I'm a grown up, I should be able to. I understand about dynamics and emotions and stuff, why can't I deal with this?'

And so, she felt that she was the odd one out, assumed there was something wrong with her, and on the occasions that she attempted to meet their banter, she felt utterly inauthentic and unable to be herself. Her coping mechanism was to withdraw, isolating herself further, and, in essence, fulfilling her perception that she did not belong.

In other circumstances, the opportunity to establish relationships is there, but what is absent are connections beyond superficial or professional levels. This was the situation for one of my interviewees in two different roles. In the first, Joanne was at the beginning of what turned out to be a brief career in teaching. She was a young academic amidst a group of over 40s, married, family men and women, with whom she could find nothing in common. At a time when she was still finding her feet, that absence of quality relationships in the workplace was very isolating:

> There were no allies. There was no real support. I was in a job where you're literally just dumped in it and go and get on with it. And I just felt completely out of place. No sense of competence and I didn't feel connected at all to any of my colleagues, you know, no friendship in the workplace. No personal connection with colleagues. Very isolated.

This scenario repeated itself in her senior role at a charitable foundation working with a team of very different minded individuals.

> They were quite conservative you know, don't drink, don't smoke, don't party. There were just so many things, just completely different people to

me. So, again it's that sense of being an outsider. I mean, nice people, don't get me wrong, but just very different life experiences, very different expectations. We got on well on a day-to-day basis, but actually trying to find connections proved to be quite difficult.

What became apparent from my conversations, and from the existing research, is that not being able to connect with people in the workplace on a personal level also means that we do not have the opportunity to be open about how we are feeling, to share our emotional experience, and feel validated, understood and cared for, which are cornerstones of intimate interactions and quality relationships.[8] These types of quality relationships are described as having high 'emotional carrying capacity,' which means we feel comfortable expressing a range of emotions and that those emotions will be understood. They also have high levels of 'tensility,' in that they will withstand setbacks, and high 'connectivity,' meaning they are tolerant of new information and challenges.[9] All of these components mean that those in these relationships feel more able to speak up about their feelings, are less cautious in their interactions and feel comfortable introducing new concerns.[10]

One of the tragic consequences of not being able to be open about experiencing a sense of not belonging is that it also means we cannot learn that we are not the only individual feeling the way that we do, and so often this perception that we are alone in our experience compounds the sense of not belonging. For Sarah, a Professor I spoke with, believing that she was the only one feeling like an outsider in her department had a significant impact on her experience. She told me "Not having anyone close to me, and not being able to confide and not having someone just to say what you are feeling, validate what I was feeling, it's normal, OK. I kept thinking it's me, it's me."

Delia's experience in her high-banter office changed dramatically when she was finally able to establish relationships where she felt safe enough to disclose how she felt.

> So, it wasn't until I got to know some of the other team a bit better that we started to share things and I was asking advice about how to deal with it. And it really wasn't until we had those discussions that I understood that I was not alone in that point of view.

Believing that we are alone in our experience can significantly compound a sense of not belonging. The perception that everyone else is doing just fine fitting in, feeling accepted and valued, only serves to accentuate the feeling of being an outsider. Learning that we are not alone in how we are feeling can be transformational, as I saw first-hand some years ago. I was facilitating an experiential leadership development programme, and my role was to observe four or five participants to see how they were behaving and interacting so I could provide them with feedback at the end of the programme. One individual I was watching looked completely detached. He was quiet and withdrawn, appeared anxious and out of his depth. For the first few hours he barely said a word. Then, during a time-out from the process one of the other participants asked whether anyone else in the group was feeling completely out of their depth. The transformation in my participant was radical. I saw a cloud lift from his face, he nodded enthusiastically, and from that moment on was engaged, much more confident and involved. In following up with that gentleman in his feedback session I learned that he did indeed feel that he was out of his depth and was not able to contribute anything, which resulted in him feeling like an outsider. The positive impact on his experience and on his behaviour of knowing he was not the only one was profound. I made a point from that day on to always inform my participants on that programme that the likelihood was that everyone at some point would be feeling like they were the only one not 'getting it.' They were not alone.

What you may read from this description is that this gentleman's sense of not belonging was related primarily to a sense of a lack of competence, that he had nothing of value to add to the group. Coupled with the fact that he had not yet established relationships which enabled him to express that, resulted in his sense of not belonging. You will also see from Joanne that her sense of not belonging during her brief teaching career involved both an absence of quality relationships and a sense that she was not competent in the role. This sense of a lack of competence, of not adding value, is the second critical component of a sense of not belonging in the workplace.

Adding value and belonging

What does it feel like to be valued? White and MacKenzie-Davey define it as "*A positive, affective response arising from confirmation, within a congruent set of criteria, of an individual's possession of the qualities on which worth or desirability depends.*"[11] This essentially translates as a positive feeling from the knowledge that we possess qualities which are considered by others to be valuable. It is again an experience that many of us will recognise in the workplace. Being praised for a report, commended for a presentation, being invited to offer our opinion, knowing that we have made a significant contribution to the thinking behind or the delivery of a project, helped a colleague to develop, a child to excel, a patient to recover or the implementation of a system to succeed. All of these experiences leave us with a warm glow, a sense of competence, value and self-worth. And they help us to feel we belong.

As we are hired by organisations to do a good job, to add value, this contributor to our sense of belonging becomes particularly important at work, and researchers have found that feeling we are making a difference, adding value, are respected, and recognised for our work is an important component of a sense of belonging in the workplace.[12, 13] Indeed, Hagerty's *Sense of Belonging Indicator*, a tool which assesses an individual's sense of belonging at work, measures two constructs: A sense of *fit* and a sense of *valued involvement*.[14]

This was also apparent across many of those individuals with whom I spoke. Clive was a manager at a large housing association. His role was to create and update policies and procedures for the management and maintenance of properties in order to meet inspection requirements. However, after the inspection came and went, the role moved to standardising procedures across regions, and it soon became apparent that the policies he was creating were seldom adhered to and the Directorate had little interest in their development or implementation. Their interest had been purely to get through the inspection. Soon afterwards, the small team that he had been working with dispersed, and he ended up feeling very isolated and invisible. He told me:

> You are fulfilling what you thought was a role – the directors had asked you to do this thing because it was important to the business. And it was important, up to a point. And then you became, over time, more and more isolated both from above and below because what you were doing was seen as less and less important or any merit. So, they were just prepared to leave you sitting there, twiddling your thumbs producing nothing of any value. Which just made you feel pretty useless. I really did go through a period where, I think the values that I thought were driving me, and the purpose of being engaged at work, it was all sort of – it all became sort of dissolved to a point where I seemed to have no purpose.

Elaine, who worked as a senior auditor, illustrated the positive version of this scenario as she discussed times when she had felt a keen sense of belonging. One of her roles involved a lot of European travel with a close-knit team, in which she felt a real sense of fit. But for Elaine, what made the difference was a director who made her and her colleagues feel valuable and important.

> You'd feel valued because you'd get recognition, not necessarily financial, but you'd get recognition just from comments. It's funny, it's a feeling of belonging. I think probably when you feel it completely, is when your opinion is asked. You are adding value, your opinions are valued, you're valued as a person.

She recalled with a smile a time when one of her Managing Directors called her out of the blue, for her opinion on an important audit:

> He said, 'Can you give me some help with this. I've got an auditor. What do you think I should do? How should I speak to them?' And I thought that's super. That's what, that's what feeling like an insider is.

Difference and belonging

The third critical component to experiencing a sense of not belonging at work is an absence of shared characteristics – actually being different in some way, from those with whom we work, or simply just feeling different.[15] Those differences which find us in a minority at work in terms of ethnicity, sexuality, gender, identity, disability or cognitive makeup receive a wealth of welcome attention from the enormously valuable body of academic and practitioner work around diversity and inclusion, which we will explore more in Chapter 7. This work aims to ensure that everyone in the workplace, irrespective of their background, receives equal opportunities, are treated with respect, and able to work in a supportive and inclusive environment. An inclusive environment is one which values difference and in which everyone feels valued, is able to contribute and able to be themselves – as we will explore in Chapter 9.

However, the differences that are found to contribute to a sense of not belonging are more wide ranging and also include differences in educational, professional or socio-economic background, as well as individual characteristics and demographics. They might involve, for example, working with a group of colleagues, as did Jason, with whom I spoke, all of whom have Oxbridge degrees, or conversely having a group of co-workers who are much less qualified than we are. The difference might involve having an unusual route to management such as that of Neil, who arrived at his role as Head of a Residential Care Home via psychology, psychotherapy and then musical therapy. Or it could simply involve being the out-spoken extravert in a team of sombre introverts.

Sarah's first experience of not belonging arose when she arrived in the UK from America. She was working as an HR Manager at a large corporation, and her cultural difference, her Americanness was a significant difference for her, and left her with a keen sense of being an outsider.

> The predominant thing was I was so different culturally. I mean you know, everything from how I dressed to how open I was and how direct I was. I'd ring my best friend in the States, and she would validate me. But people in this country are so different in how they behave that I kept feeling it was clearly just me.

What is important to these differences is that they are salient and significant to us, irrespective of whether those around us are even aware of them. These *perceived* differences can become our defining focus, particularly if complemented by a lack of relationships or sense of value and impact a sense of not belonging by creating a distance between 'us' and 'them' and placing us *outside* of the group to whom we want to belong.

These perceived differences can also impact our sense of adding value, as they can be interpreted by us as having, often erroneous, implications for our status in comparison to others, and can impact evaluations that both we and others make about us. Being old, young, black, homosexual, from a different educational or socio-economic background can provide signals as to our inferiority or superiority as well as our 'fit.'[16, 17] These status characteristics as such give rise to 'expectation states' – expectations, both that we and others hold, about how we will perform and behave. They can be based on both conscious or unconscious bias, informed by stereotypes and beliefs we hold about people based on their characteristics which can be either inside or outside of our own conscious awareness.[18]

Examples of these assumptions were demonstrated in numerous research studies in the 1960s and 1970s.[19] One study found that when people's actual performance was controlled for, evaluations by women of male performance were more positive than evaluations by women of female performance.[20] Similar studies found white adult's evaluations of black children's performance to be determined by ethnicity irrespective of actual performance.[21] These assumptions continue, and are all around us today, evidenced in outdated ideas, for example, as to whether women can be tough negotiators, men can be nursery carers, older generations can program computers and design apps or female students can excel in STEM subjects.[22] They are implicit too in the racial discrimination experienced by black minorities and fought against hard by the Black Lives Matter movement, which demonstrates the impact of these biases on how we are treated, respected, and valued. In the workplace too, when these biases are held by others, they can have enormously detrimental implications for recruitment decisions, academic journeys and career paths. And when we ourselves are aware of these biases they can impact our sense of 'otherness,' and our sense of belonging. We will return to this in Chapter 7.

Critically however, the assumptions of others can also impact our self-efficacy, our *self*-perceptions, beliefs and confidence in our own capabilities.[23, 24] This has been empirically demonstrated in numerous studies, including, for example, a study of male US Navy students which explored the impact of hierarchical status on decision-making processes. In this study, participants were either partnered with a low-status partner, a 'seaman' or a high-status partner a 'lieutenant.' They were then asked to determine which side of a checkerboard contained the most white squares. Following their initial decision, they reviewed the decision of their partner and then offered their final judgement. The study found that those who partnered with the lieutenant were significantly *more* likely to defer to the lieutenant's decision and those partnered with the seaman significantly *less* likely to defer to the seaman's decisions.[25] These findings have been replicated with different characteristics, including, for example, educational background, whereby those with lower status educational backgrounds have been found to be more likely to be influenced in their decision-making than those with higher educational status.[26] As such, different status characteristics not only result in us feeling a sense of difference, but also impact our sense of capability and value and can impact the way that we behave and the choices that we make.

Over 30 years ago, one of my closest friends took the brave decision to apply to Cambridge University to study English Literature. She had every right to attend as she was, and still is one of the brightest, studious and academically gifted people I know. But she was from a State school and a working-class family, a background that was reflected in her sans-serif accent. But she refused to let the potential biases of the Admissions Board determine her academic path, made her application and was accepted. But those working-class roots, and the assumptions and expectations that she believed were entwined with them undermined her sense of acceptance and capability during her university years and whispered in her ear at the start of her teaching career at a Grammar School. Whilst they failed to stop her achieving, they made the journey a significantly greater challenge.

For Jason, with whom I spoke, his sense of difference had a profound impact on his own perception of his capabilities and affected how he behaved and performed throughout his career in the public sector. For Jason, his 'difference' was both educational and social. He was surrounded by colleagues with Cambridge and Oxford degrees, some of whom came from distinctly middle-class backgrounds. He told me:

> I always felt looked down on. Not that it's a class thing, but a various mixture of things, class, education, you know, knowledge, whatever it might be. I always felt that a lot of people were looking down on me. And so, I behaved in a way that was subservient. I would adopt a low status, they would always adopt a very high status. I was very deferential, not challenging them when they said stupid things. It also meant I didn't have to push myself too much and I could limit the scope of my ambitions or limit the scope of what I felt I should be doing, and that just fed into a sort of growing negative feeling about my abilities.

In this way, the assumptions and expectations that 'difference' can create can quite easily perpetuate a sense of not belonging. As we will explore in Chapter 4, behaving in a subservient and deferential manner, or withdrawing or disengaging at work, limits the value that we can add to our teams and organisations, and so can further undermine our sense of adding value, and as such, our sense of belonging.

Organisational culture

The final factor to consider in this chapter is that of the organisations for whom we work. Organisational practices, structures and cultures can have a significant influence on whether a sense of not belonging is fostered, developed and maintained. This can manifest in a number of ways, one of which is working for an organisation or institution whose values are at odds with our own, with a lack of alignment between personal and organisational values inhibiting a sense of belonging and leading to sense of psychological disengagement and alienation.[27, 28]

A key scholar of organisational culture, Edgar Schein, identifies three layers of culture: Artefacts which include structures, practices and processes and visibly represent the underlying values and assumptions of an organisation; beliefs and values, the espoused beliefs which are used to validate patterns of behaviour and guide choices in ways of working, and determine how individuals act, speak and interpret their organisation; and underlying assumptions, the unconscious, implicit beliefs and expectations shared by members of the organisation, such as perceptions, thoughts and feelings.[29] Given that these core values and underlying assumptions are both deeply rooted and ingrained, and key indicators of what is right and wrong, misalignment with these core values is likely to result in a cognitive dissonance and a perception of not belonging. For example, if corporate responsibility is an important personal value but your company refuses to implement fair trade policies, adhere to the Modern Slavery Act, or work towards being carbon neutral, this is likely to create a sense of disconnection, a lack of fit and belonging, particularly if you do not have good relationships with others in the office to share your concerns and validate your views.

This was the experience of Nathan when he was working as an HR Specialist at a large financial services firm, which, through rapid growth, developed a culture that did not fit with the values that encouraged him into his profession:

> When I came into the organisation it was a mid-sized organisation, growing very fast. We were 3000 employees then, and at the peak of it, we were about 16,000. I was part of that process when the organisation grew really well. And then there was a period when we had to lay off a lot of people and being on the HR and OD side of the business it was tough on us, because it was a challenging thing to do. And at that time, I developed a general dissatisfaction. I realised that it had a lot to do with the culture of the organisation and the response to very challenging external, environmental issues. It was not very appropriate. There's a central discourse that human resource managers should think like business managers. And that's precisely the discourse I was part of. But I also realised that if everyone starts to think like business managers then who will think like HR? And I realised that I

was getting away from, or we were getting away from what we ought to be doing, and that somehow created the feeling of, you know not belonging, not only to the organisation, but to the profession.

Clive also found that as his role shifted at the housing association, he started drifting away from any real connection to his personal values which were once aligned with his work:

I took a deliberate decision to go into public housing because one of my grandfathers had had houses that he let at peppercorn rent down in south London, years ago. I'd always had an interest, because of that, in social housing. I could see the purpose of it and why it was needed. So, I chose that line of work because I had some belief in its purpose. For the first eighteen years I felt I was actually engaging in delivering exactly that. That was my driver, it was my focus point. But the more the word 'compliance' was bandied about, the more the businesses said, 'well we're in competition with each other. We want to show we've got a better way of doing this, that we're the smarter cookies,'. You can't square that corner. I wasn't connected any more to the purpose and there was no path back to it.

What we also know is particularly critical to belonging in the workplace is psychological safety. Psychological safety, which we will explore in detail in Chapter 8, was coined as a key organisational concept by Amy Edmondson in 1999 and has grown in importance and attracted a great deal of research ever since. Edmondson defines it as an individual's perception that the team environment is safe for interpersonal risk taking.[30] It describes environments in which employees feel safe to speak up, to offer their thoughts and ideas without fear of judgement or ridicule. This means that they can make themselves heard, add their voice and contribute value to their organisations, supporting the development of this critical component of belonging. In these environments it is also okay to ask questions, to demonstrate vulnerability and to need help or ask for support. Psychological safety has also been found to play an important role in supporting those from ethnic minorities to feel valued in their organisations.[31]

When I worked in a particularly psychologically safe environment, shouting a question across the office, getting some insight or help with something new or disagreeing with an established process was completely acceptable. With that job I felt entirely like I belonged because I was able to be heard, did not have to hide my occasional absence of knowledge and could constructively contribute to how the team functioned. But if I had not felt I belonged I would have been able to voice how I felt, get support for that and perhaps learn that others also felt the way I did, helping me to feel less of an outsider.

Organisational culture had an impact on the experience of many of those with whom I spoke. Sarah worked for a few years in a large technology firm which through fear of being in the bottom 10% of performers fostered a strong competitive and individualistic culture. There was no sense of being part of a team or pulling together. Rather, everyone kept their knowledge, skills or experience to themselves, protecting their own value, and no one dared demonstrate any weakness or vulnerability, or share their concerns. Similarly, the very masculine and assertive culture that Delia found herself in, one that neither fitted with her values nor her own way of behaving, also made it difficult for her to make herself heard, or feel comfortable enough to voice her opinions. She told me:

> Banter was the currency of that company. And it became an excuse for just behaving badly eventually. It started off quite funny and quite enjoyable and, you have to give back as good as you get, otherwise you don't fit in the gang, you don't get respected, and you don't get liked. But I felt put down with the bantery type of thing, it was a mild, a subtle form of bullying, or not so subtle form of bullying. So, I withdrew. But then when you withdraw you don't get noticed and you don't get acknowledged, and you don't have your ideas heard, and you lose power when you do that, that was my experience. I lost power. And I lost prominence.

The withdrawal that Delia found herself forced into in order to protect herself from the culture flew completely in the face of who she was – she was a bubbly, outgoing, extravert. And so, one of the consequences of this culture was inauthenticity, and an inability to be herself. This was also true for Lydia who found herself being overly assertive in order to have her voice heard in the competitive and aggressive culture of the law firm for whom she worked. In fact, as we will explore in detail in Chapter 4, inauthentic behaviours are a regular and self-defeating response to a sense of not belonging as we attempt to protect ourselves or find a way to fit in. But what these acts of inauthenticity also do is impact our sense of having a clear and coherent self-concept – they undermine what we know about ourselves, and it is this impact on our sense of self that is at the heart of the significance of a sense of not belonging and is to that which we will now turn.

Notes

1 Gill, R., Levine, N., & Pitt, D. C. (1999). Leadership and organizations for the new millennium. *Journal of Leadership Studies*, 5(4), 46–59. https://doi.org/10.1177/107179199900500405
2 Waller, L. (2020). Fostering a sense of belonging in the workplace: Enhancing well-being and a positive and coherent sense of self. *The Palgrave Handbook of Workplace Well-Being*, 1–27. https://doi.org/10.1007/978-3-030-02470-3_83-1
3 Reis, H. T. (1990). The role of intimacy in interpersonal relations. *Journal of Social and Clinical Psychology*, 9, 15–30. https://doi.org/10.1521/jscp.1990.9.1.15

4 Belle, S. M., Burley, D. L., & Long, S. D. (2015). Where do I belong? high-intensity teleworkers' experience of organizational belonging. *Human Resource Development International*, 18(1), 76–96. http://doi:10.1080/13678868.2014.979006
5 Waller, L. (2020). Fostering a sense of belonging in the workplace: Enhancing well-being and a positive and coherent sense of self. *The Palgrave Handbook of Workplace Well-Being*, 1–27. https://doi.org/10.1007/978-3-030-02470-3_83-1
6 Somers, M. (1999). Development and preliminary validation of a measure of belongingness. (Unpublished Ph.D.). Temple University, Philadelphia. http://doi:10.1037/e345822004-001
7 Reiss, H. T. (1990). The role of intimacy in interpersonal relations. *Journal of Social and Clinical Psychology*, 9, 15–30. https://doi.org/10.1521/jscp.1990.9.1.15
8 Reiss, H. T. (1990). The role of intimacy in interpersonal relations. *Journal of Social and Clinical Psychology*, 9, 15–30. https://doi.org/10.1521/jscp.1990.9.1.15
9 Dutton, J. E., & Heaphy, E. D. (2003). The power of high-quality relationships at work. In K. S. Cameron, J. E. Dutton & R. E. Quinn (Eds.) *Positive organizational scholarship*. San Francisco, CA: Berrett-Koehler Publishers, 263–278.
10 Carmeli, A., Brueller, D., & Dutton, J. E. (2009). Learning behaviours in the workplace: The role of high-quality interpersonal relationships and psychological safety. *Systems Research and Behavioral Science*, 26(1), 81–98. https://doi.org/10.1002/sres.932
11 White, M., & MacKenzie-Davey, K. (2003). Feeling valued at work? A qualitative study of corporate training consultants. *Career Development International*, 8(5), 228–234, p. 228. https://doi.org/10.1108/13620430310497395
12 McClure, J. P., & Brown, J. M. (2008). Belonging at work. *Human Resource Development International*, 11(1), 3–17. http://doi:10.1080/13678860701782261
13 Levett-Jones, T., & Lathlean, J. (2009). The ascent to competence conceptual framework: An outcome of a study of belongingness. *Journal of Clinical Nursing*, 18(20), 2870–2879. http://doi:10.1111/j.1365-2702.2008.02593.x
14 Hagerty, B. M. K., Lynch-Sauer, J., Patusky, K. L., Bouwsema, M., & Collier, P. (1992). Sense of belonging: A vital mental health concept. *Archives of Psychiatric Nursing*, 6, 172–177. http://doi:10.1016/0883-9417(92)90028-h
15 Hagerty, B. M. K. et al. (1992). Sense of belonging: A vital mental health concept. *Archives of Psychiatric Nursing*, 6, 172–177. https://doi.org/10.1016/0883-9417(92)90028-H
16 Berger, J., Rosenholtz, S. J., & Zelditch Jr, M. (1980). Status organizing processes. *Annual Review of Sociology*, 6(1), 479–508. http://doi:10.1146/annurev.so.06.080180.002403
17 Benoit-Smullyan, E. (1944). Status, status types, and status interrelations. *American Sociological Review*, 9, 151–161. https://doi.org/10.2307/2086307
18 Kahneman, D., Lovallo, D., & Sibony, O. (2011). The big idea: Before you make that big decision. *Harvard Business Review*, 89(6), 50–60.
19 Ward, D., & Balswick, J. (1978). Strong men and virtuous women: A content analysis of sex roles stereotypes. *Pacific Sociological Review*, 21(1), 45–53. https://doi.org/10.2307/1388866
20 Goldberg, P. (1968). Are women prejudiced against women? *Transaction*, 5, 28–30. https://doi.org/10.1007/BF03180445

21 Coates, B. (1972). White adult behavior toward black and white children. *Child Development*, 43(1), 43–54. https://doi.org/10.2307/1127878
22 Lavy, V., & Sand, E. (2015). On the origins of gender human capital gaps: Short and long term consequences of teachers' stereotypical biases. *National Bureau of Economic Research*. https://doi.10.3386/w20909
23 Tajfel, H., & Turner, J. C. (1986). The social identity theory of intergroup behavior. *Psychology of Intergroup Relations*, 5, 7–24.
24 Berger, J., Rosenholtz, S. J., & Zelditch Jr., M. (1980). Status organizing processes. *Annual Review of Sociology*, 6(1), 479–508. https://doi.org/10.1146/annurev.so.06.080180.002403
25 Driskell, J. E., & Salas, E. (1991). Group decision making under stress. *Journal of Applied Psychology*, 76, 473–478. https://doi.org/10.1037/0021-9010.76.3.473
26 Moore, J. (1968). Status and influence in small group inter- actions. *Sociometry*, 31(March), 47–63. https://doi.org/10.2307/2786479
27 Belle, S. M., Burley, D. L., & Long, S. D. (2015). Where do I belong? high-intensity teleworkers' experience of organizational belonging. *Human Resource Development International*, 18(1), 76–96. https://doi:10.1080/13678868.2014.979006
28 Levett-Jones, T., & Lathlean, J. (2009). The ascent to competence conceptual framework: An outcome of a study of belongingness. *Journal of Clinical Nursing*, 18(20), 2870–2879. https://doi:10.1111/j.1365-2702.2008.02593.x
29 Schein, E. H. (1985). *Organisational culture and leadership*. San Francisco, CA: Jossey-Bass.
30 Edmondson, A. C. (1999). Psychological safety and learning behavior in work teams. *Administration Science Quarterly*, 44(2), 350–383. https://doi:10.2307/2666999
31 Singh, B., Winkel, D. E., & Selvarajan, T. T. (2013). Managing diversity at work: Does psychological safety hold the key to racial differences in employee performance? *Journal of Occupational and Organizational Psychology*, 86(2), 242–263. https://doi.org/10.1111/joop.12015

3
Belonging and well-being

> I was trying to question what's happening. My initial reaction was that there is something that is wrong with me. And that needs to be corrected. Why is it happening? Everything is OK. Everything is fine. And yet I'm having this feeling. So, there must be something that needs to be fixed.
>
> – Nathan, HR Consultant

You should now have a good insight into why a sense of belonging is so important to us, and what sort of situations, environments and factors support and undermine its development in the workplace. From your own experience you will likely too have a keen appreciation for how it *feels* to belong. That dopamine-induced warm sense of self-assurance, confidence, contentment that we experience when we feel we belong to a group. When we know, profoundly, that we are accepted, wanted, needed. That we bring something valuable, even unique to our relationships, teams and work.

You may also know from your own experience, and no doubt have a sense from the accounts I have described in the previous chapter of how it might feel to believe we do *not* belong. This insight is critical to us as leaders in part because it is incumbent upon us to ensure that our employees feel good about themselves at work – have positive psychological well-being. But also, as we will explore in the next chapter, how it feels to not belong is also fundamental to how we behave and perform in our roles.

In order to explore this meaningfully we need to focus on how it feels to *not* belong, rather than *to* belong. This is because a sense of *not* belonging is not simply the polar opposite of a sense *of* belonging, in much the same way that our experience of something going well is often less significant to us than something going badly. Enjoyment of the sense of achievement when we deliver a perfect presentation, are commended for an insightful report, are offered

DOI: 10.4324/9781003108849-5

a promotion – compared to the critical examination, negative self-talk and soul-searching that accompanies the messed-up speech, the error-ridden paper and the job going to someone else – belonging is something we value, we enjoy and embrace; *not* belonging is something we analyse and critique. And when we critique, we often turn the microscope on ourselves and find the cause within us – and it is this self-criticism, this negative self-perception that both magnifies and galvanises the emotional and psychological impact of a sense of not belonging.

Belonging and our sense of self

What I discovered through my research, and other scholars through their investigations have intimated, is that core to a sense of not belonging, central to the significant and detrimental impact that it can have, is its capacity to undermine our sense of self. Feeling that we do not belong, as will be explored below, can diminish our self-esteem and self-worth, can leave us questioning our self-efficacy and confusing our understanding of who we are.

So, what do we mean by *the self*? There are very many conceptualisations of self-concept and there will be many books on the shelves that focus on this topic alone. But brought down to its bare bones, self-concept is essentially our view of ourselves – the knowledge and information we hold about ourselves, including our traits, our values, our memories and experience.[1] If I were to try to capture my self-concept, I would describe myself as an outgoing introvert (if that is not an oxymoron), intuitive, determined, driven, passionate, gung-ho and a little controlling. My most important values are inclusivity, compassion, family and empathy. I am motivated by developing myself and others, helping them to have the self-esteem and confidence to be the best they can be and to feel unique and valued. That, in a nutshell, is my self-concept.

What is particularly relevant to belonging is that as well as this personal knowledge, the self-concept also incorporates a relational and collective component which is determined by who we are in relation to others. My collective sense of self as such, would be a white, English, heterosexual, woman. In terms of my relational self, I am a mother because I have daughters, a wife because I have a husband; I am the quiet one when out with my extrovert husband, and the chatty one when out with some of my more introverted friends. I am the super busy, professional school mum next to the stay-at-home mothers from the playground, and the chilled out working-from home mum next to the high-flying corporate types dashing into London at 6am every morning. As such, who we 'are,' who we consider ourselves to be, who others consider us to be is socially determined by our interactions with others and how we compare ourselves to them, and contextually determined through the social roles we hold and the groups to which we belong.[2]

As well as being determined by how we compare with others, our self-concept is also determined by what we *believe* others think of us. The model of the 'looking-glass self' proposes that our self-concept reflects our own belief about how we appear to others and comprises: Our perception of how we appear to others; our perception of other's judgement of that appearance; and an element of either pride or shame, depending on that perceived judgement.[3] As such, I may appear as the quiet one with my husband's friends but believe that I am judged as the dull and disengaged one and feel therefore a sense of shame. Alternatively, I may appear as the well-educated one in other groups, believe I am judged as clever, and therefore feel a sense of pride. What we believe others think of us therefore informs what we think of ourselves, and how we feel about ourselves. *They think, therefore I am.*

These propositions, however, are also grounded in research which has found a causal relationship between what we think of ourselves and what we think others think of us – that is to say, it has demonstrated that what we think others think *informs* what we think and not the other way around.[4] Interestingly however, research frequently fails to find a relationship between what we think others think and what they *actually* think.[5] The assumptions we make, the seemingly often-erroneous perceptions we have can therefore serve to unjustly undermine our own sense of self – a thought we will return to in Chapter 10.

As interesting as all this is, what does it have to do with belonging? If our self-concept is informed by both how we compare ourselves to others and how we believe others judge us, having a sense that we do not belong, are not accepted, and valued by others is very likely to have a detrimental impact on what we think of ourselves, undermining our self-concept and our self-esteem, as indeed was found in my and others' research.

Self-efficacy, competence and self-belief

One component of the self-concept that is undermined by a sense of not belonging is our self-efficacy, the belief that we can be successful in future tasks. It is our sense of competence and confidence in our abilities.[6] Professor Tracy Levett-Jones, Director of the Research Centre for Health Professional Education at The University of Newcastle and Judith Lathlean, Professor of Health Research at University of Southampton have researched the sense of belonging for student nurses for many years. They articulate belonging as a process, and through their studies they developed the Ascent to Competence Conceptual

Belonging and well-being

Framework, an adaptation of Maslow's Hierarchy of Needs that suggests that we begin at the stage of safety and security, and progress through the stages of belongingness, self-concept, learning and finally, at the pinnacle of their pyramid, competence, which they describe as "The need to become a competent, confident, efficacious, and capable professional with a passion for, and commitment to patient-centred care."[7]

Believing that we do not belong however can be retold in our minds to mean we are not good enough and we do not add value. As such, we question our competence and our ability to do the job. Our sense of who we are is destabilised and self-doubt in our decisions and judgement ignited. Coupling this with the often-held perception that others are more competent than we are places 'others' together and us further on the outside.[8]

Lydia, for example, was a very capable legal professional whose sense of not belonging undermined her confidence in her abilities. This lack of confidence carried over into new roles fuelling her negative self-perception as she held back from contributing and making decisions.

> [I had] no confidence to do my job. I was very wary of the partners and the environment. And I was scared to make decisions actually. So, whereas before I'd been able to do my job absolutely fine, I remember getting to this law firm and then thinking, oh my god I can't even do my job now. I questioned, I remember questioning myself a lot about what I was doing, and whether I was good enough.

Lydia's scenario illustrates what so often is the case with a sense of not belonging at work – our undermined self-confidence results in us fulfilling our fears – we believe we are not competent and we therefore behave as such.

Self-esteem

If self-efficacy is the cognitive aspect of our self-concept – our perception of our abilities – self-esteem is the evaluative component of the self-concept. It refers to how we feel about ourselves, whether we judge ourselves, or aspects of ourselves negatively or positively. Our self-esteem is categorised as trait and state as well as global and situational. Trait self-esteem is our typical level of self-esteem that we have in regard to most parts of ourselves most of the time, and global self-esteem refers to how we typically feel about ourselves in most situations. State self-esteem on the other hand refers to how we feel about certain aspects of ourselves, and situational self-esteem varies depending on the situation we are in.[9, 10] For example, we may have a good opinion about our social skills, but not our intellect; we may feel good about who we are as a colleague, but not who we are as a parent; feel proud of ourselves when in the gym, but not in the classroom; when amongst our friends, but not our student peers. Again, different situations, different people, and how we see ourselves in relation to others impacts our self-esteem. Therefore, believing that others do not accept and value us at work will have a keen impact on our own self-esteem, as has been consistently found in research.

In fact, the significance of this relationship is considered to be so strong that Mark Leary, through his *Sociometer Hypothesis*, argues that self-esteem is actually an internal gauge that alerts us to a threat to our acceptance, inclusion and value to others and motivates us to behave in ways that will address this threat.[11] Essentially, he believes that the function – the purpose of self-esteem – is to make us aware that our inclusion is under threat, encourage us to change our behaviour and as such, ensure we remain included, safe and survive. In much the same way as the release of dopamine when we are connected and contributing real value to an important meeting is telling us to continue speaking up and offering our opinions, the feeling and emotional pain of low self-esteem when we are not invited to join the lunch, the meeting, the conversation, is telling us to work out how we need to behave in order to be accepted or protected from further pain. Cognitive and behavioural responses that we will explore in depth in the next chapter.

Mark Leary's proposition is well supported by both laboratory studies, which have found significant relationships between exclusion, rejection and self-esteem[12, 13, 14, 15, 16] as well as studies in organisations where feeling socially excluded, unappreciated and unaccepted by others has been found to be related to diminished self-worth, a sense of inferiority, low self-esteem, self-blame and inadequacy.[17, 18]

In my research, the impact on self-esteem was core to the significance and negative impact of a sense of not belonging. What is critical is the meaning that we place on having a sense of not belonging – what we believe it says about who we were as a person, that undermines our self-esteem. We tell ourselves 'I don't feel I add value, that I matter, I am different, therefore there must be something wrong with me'; 'I feel depressed and anxious, I must be weak and irrational'; 'I tried to fit in therefore I am inauthentic' and 'I must do well at work, but I feel I don't belong, so I am a failure.'

Neil, who was a very successful CEO of a health institution and had experienced a sense of not belonging on many occasions throughout his career blamed himself for not being accepted at work:

> I beat myself up quite a lot about it. Because I blame myself. That's the other aspect of it for not belonging, it's because of something I've said or something I've done, or the way I've behaved or something. And you end up having a real downer on yourself.

For Neil, as with others, having a sense of not belonging undermined his self-esteem through the belief that there was something about him that meant he was not 'acceptable.'

However, a sense of not belonging can also undermine self-esteem through the very fact that the experience occurs – it can instigate a perception of weakness, perhaps shame, that we do not have the resilience, the strength to deal with the situation we are in. For Sandra, Head of Finance for a Government Department, not fitting in was a familiar experience for her, and one for which she completely subsumed the blame. She told me:

> I feel like I should be able to do it. I feel like there's something missing. Like there is a linking thing that's missing. Other people can do this, and I can't. That's a sort of a deficiency in a way, isn't it?

Delia similarly considered those who were able to fit in as being more *whole human beings*, and Nathan believed there was something about him that *needs to be fixed*. These examples illustrate a substantial impact of a sense of not belonging on fundamental elements of our self-concept – of our 'rightness' as a person.

This self-perception becomes further compounded by a concern about how others perceive us. As explored earlier, what we think of ourselves is greatly impacted by what we *think* others think of us – and a sense of not belonging frequently involves the belief that we are judged as incompetent, weak, inferior or plain unlikeable – perceptions that we believe either cause us to not be accepted (I'm not liked therefore I'm not accepted), or are in response to what we assume are our visible reactions to not belonging (others judge me because I feel vulnerable or retreat).

One of the oft-felt concerns associated with not belonging is a perception that we lack competence and credibility in the eyes of others. At the time that I spoke with him Jason was an experienced consultant but began his career in the public sector. At that time, his sense of not belonging was triggered by a sense of difference – of not having the same educational and career background as his peers. This led him to believe that others did not see him as either credible or competent.

> I always felt that a lot of people were looking down on me. So, I'd be in meetings and just feel that these people didn't actually rate me in any shape or form because I wasn't one of them, and I didn't know enough really to buy my place at the table.

Not belonging for so many is associated with a genuine concern that we are not respected, not taken seriously, seen as incompetent, stupid, idiots even, by those with whom we work.

I am often asked whether sense of not belonging is the same thing as imposter syndrome. And whilst similar, it is this assumption that we are being judged poorly by others that distinguishes one from the other. Imposter syndrome, or imposter phenomenon, was first identified in 1978 by psychologists Pauline Clance and Suzanne Imes in their research with high achieving women. They defined it as "an internal experience of intellectual phoniness."[19] It is a sense that we have only achieved our successes and reached where we are in our organisations through luck and serendipity. A belief that we do not actually deserve to be here, and that at any moment we will be 'found out' as being incapable. Whilst first identified in successful women, it is now understood to affect many of us, anyone who struggles to internalise and take responsibility for their own success. A review in 2011 estimated that approximately 70% of us have experienced imposter phenomenon at some point in our lives,[20] and as such it may be an experience that resonates with you.

Whilst there are significant overlaps, the key distinction between a sense of not belonging and imposter syndrome is that 'imposters' are concerned that they will be found out, that is, they believe that others think they are competent and credible, whilst they themselves do not. When we feel we do not belong however, we fear that others share our perception of lack of competence, or indeed consider us to be incompetent and not adding value, even if we believe ourselves that we do.

Coherent sense of self

What research has also discovered is that a sense of not belonging can also present a *conflict* in our sense of self which emerges both through the lack of fit between how we *think and feel* when we believe we do not belong and how we normally think and feel, and also through our inability to be fully ourselves and authentic at work.[21]

As I have already described, having a sense of not belonging at work often brings about feelings of being vulnerable, of being weak or incompetent. If, sadly, this is what we generally think about ourselves, that we are incompetent, vulnerable or weak, if this is our global and stable self-perception, feeling that we do not belong at work, whilst still a negative experience, is unlikely to be quite as significant or intense, because it is familiar, it is what we anticipate, it is what we know about ourselves. If I know that I am self-conscious and a little quiet in senior leadership meetings I know what to expect. I know I will listen well, respond if spoken to, but probably keep my thoughts to myself because I tend to feel a little out of my depth. Frustrating perhaps, but concerning, probably not. But if I find myself becoming intimidated and self-conscious in meetings that I normally feel confident in, if I find I am doubting myself, withholding what I normally consider to be valuable contributions, this frustration turns to perhaps fear, confusion, a sense of irrationality. It is no longer just the situation that is causing me concern, but how I am feeling, how I am thinking. 'This is not me; it conflicts with what I know about myself' – it creates a cognitive dissonance which feels uncomfortable and distressing.[22]

The reason this self-conflict is so challenging to us is because the conflict is between deep-structured fundamental beliefs about ourselves. It is not simply a matter of a conflict of identities such as the behavioural and cognitive demands of being a mother versus those of being a company director, or indeed between the way we interact and behave with one member of our team who needs clear direction, and the way we behave towards a self-directed, independent member. Those are adaptations that we frequently need to make to cope with competing demands or to be an effective and responsive leader. But believing ourselves to be both vulnerable and resilient, incompetent and credible, extroverted and introverted creates a paradox, a cognitive dissonance between conflicting thoughts about fundamental aspects of our self-concept, resulting in self-doubt, confusion, and also undermining our self-esteem.[23]

Sandra, who worked for the Government, illustrated the impact of this conflict well. She was the only person that I spoke with who also often felt that she did not belong outside of work. Feeling that she did not fit in to certain social groups was a frequent and anticipated experience. And when she talked to me about her sense of not belonging at work there was little intensity in her description, but instead a calm resignation, as you will no doubt note in her words:

> I've never you know, in social situations and things outside of work, I don't necessarily feel like I fit in. I'm a middle child, and I felt like an outsider I think partly through my childhood…it's not really only in a work environment, but I think I've felt like I don't fit in to a number of the work environments that I've been in in my working life. I don't know whether that's, I suppose I don't know whether that's me, or the working environment. I suspect it's me, but there you are.

What research also tells us is that a sense of not belonging impacts our ability to be ourselves at work, to be comfortable in our skin, and be true and authentic representations of who we are.[24, 25] This arises from the perception that who we are does not fit, is not accepted, is not valued, and so, we try to be something and someone different, to behave how we believe others want us to behave and present ourselves in ways that we believe others want to see and will accept. One of the most common responses is to conform – to go along with other's opinions, decisions, express appropriate emotions, or attitudes, wear appropriate clothes, in order to be accepted. According to Doctor Patricia Hewlin's Facades of Conformity theory, these attitudes are not actually internalised – we do not *change* what we think and believe, we just pretend to.[26] As authenticity is about being able to behave in ways which are consistent with our beliefs, values and true selves,[27] these facades of conformity significantly undermine this and our sense of a coherent self-concept. Something we will return to in the next chapter.

Mood and emotion

Given the above, it will be no surprise to learn that a sense of not belonging at work also has a big impact on our emotional and mental well-being. Feeling we do not belong has been found in my research and others' to be associated with two of our most common and damaging mental health challenges today – anxiety and depression.[28, 29] Feeling fearful of the intensity of the experience, of the confusion and turmoil it creates, as well as the impact our emotional state might have on our ability to do our jobs results in feelings of anxiety and vulnerability. And in a similar way, feeling we do not belong, are not accepted and valued leads to feelings of depression, desperation, emotional exhaustion and emotional vulnerability.

What also emerged from the conversations that I had was that the significance and intensity of this emotional experience was due to the accompanying confusion and inner turmoil that having those feelings ignited. In a way, what is more damaging is not how we feel, but how we *feel* about how we feel. We become concerned about our emotional control, our distorted thinking, the irrationality of how we are feeling and our seeming inability to make things better. Lydia, my legal professional expressed this sense of confusion, turmoil and ultimately self-blame:

> Actually it just felt messy. Messy and depressing, and what the hell is going on? I don't like this, and I don't understand it. Why does no one else feel like this, why is it just me? I suppose I almost felt like there was something wrong. And when I say something wrong, I mean, that there was something wrong with me. Why was I struggling with this so much? Why was I feeling so miserable and down? And why was everyone, why me, why, what's wrong with me?

According to *Attribution Theory*, this self-blame results in self-focused emotions.[30] The theory proposes that our attributions, including those of causality – who or what we blame for an event – determine the type of emotional response we have. As such, internalising the cause of not belonging or how we *respond* to not belonging will result in emotions such as shame, guilt or embarrassment. For example, if I were to be involved in a car crash which I believed was caused by the other driver, I would likely feel angry and my emotions would be directed at them, whereas if I felt that I was responsible the same experience would cause my emotions to be directed at myself, and I would likely feel guilt, shame or embarrassment.

However, the self-directed focus of our emotions does not account for the intensity and significance of the emotion that so often accompanies a sense of not belonging. What accounts for that is the fact that it is not our actions or behaviour that we blame for our not belonging, but it is who *we are*, who we are as a person, that we blame. This, according to *Self-Conscious Affect Theory*[31] results in the more damaging emotions such as shame. To take the above analogy further, if I believe the car crash was due to my actions in pulling out in front of an oncoming car, I am likely to feel guilty. But if I believe I am responsible because I am foolish, lazy, inconsiderate or just plain irresponsible I am likely to feel shame.

Therefore, the way we *feel* about not belonging impacts our very sense of self, self-esteem and self-worth because we believe that how we feel indicates a fault, a deficiency in who we are, for which we feel ashamed. It is these attributions, these often-erroneous interpretations and perceptions that are at the heart of the cyclical and perpetuating nature of the experience. We will return to these in the final chapter of this book.

Notes

1 Kihlstrom, J. F., & Cantor, N. (1984). Mental representations of the self. In *Advances in experimental social psychology*, vol. 17. Cambridge, MA: Academic Press, 1–47. https://doi:10.1016/s0065-2601(08)60117-3
2 Brewer, M., & Gardner, W. L. (1996). What is this "we"? Levels of collective identity and self-representation. *Journal of Personality and Social Psychology*, 71, 83–93. https://doi:10.1037/0022-3514.71.1.83
3 Shrauger, J. S., & Schoeneman, T. J. (1999). Symbolic interactionist view of self-concept: Through the looking glass darkly. In R. F. Baumeister (Ed.) *The self in social psychology*. New York: Psychology Press, 25–42. https://doi:10.1037/0033-2909.86.3.549
4 Manis, M. (1955). Social interaction and the self-concept. *Journal of Abnormal and Social Psychology*, 51, 362–370. https://doi.org/10.1037/h0040129
5 Walhood, D. S., & Klopfer, W. G. (1971). Congruence between self-concept and public image. *Journal of Consulting and Clinical Psychology*, 37, 148–150. https://doi.org/10.1037/h0031282
6 Bandura, A. (1997). *Self-efficacy: The exercise of control*. New York: Freeman.

7 Levett-Jones, T., & Lathlean, J. (2009). The ascent to competence conceptual framework: An outcome of a study of belongingness. *Journal of Clinical Nursing*, 18(20), 2870–2879. https://doi:10.1111/j.1365-2702.2008.02593.x
8 Waller, L. (2020). Fostering a sense of belonging in the workplace: Enhancing well-being and a positive and coherent sense of self. In S. Dhiman (Ed.) *The Palgrave handbook of workplace well-being*. Cham: Palgrave Macmillan, 341–367.
9 Leary, M. R., Tambor, E. S., Terdal, S. K., & Downs, D. L. (1995b). Self-esteem as an interpersonal monitor: The sociometer hypothesis. *Journal of Personality and Social Psychology*, 68, 518–530. https://doi:10.1037//0022-3514.68.3.518
10 Rosenberg, M., Schooler, C., Schoenbach, C., & Rosenberg, F. (1995). Global self-esteem and specific self-esteem: Different concepts, different outcomes. *American Sociological Review*, 60, 141–156. https://doi.org/10.2307/2096350
11 Leary, M. R. (2005). Sociometer theory and the pursuit of relational value: Getting to the root of self-esteem, *European Review of Social Psychology*, 16(1), 75–111. https://doi:10.1080/10463280540000007
12 Leary, M. R., Tambor, E. S., Terdal, S. K., & Downs, D. L. (1995b). Self-esteem as an interpersonal monitor: The sociometer hypothesis. *Journal of Personality and Social Psychology*, 68, 518–530. https://doi:10.1037//0022-3514.68.3.518.
13 Leary, M. R., Haupt, A. L., Strausser, K. S., & Chokel, J. T. (1998). Calibrating the sociometer: The relationship between interpersonal appraisals and state self-esteem. *Journal of Personality and Social Psychology*, 74, 1290–1299. https://doi:10.1037//0022-3514.74.5.1290
14 Leary, M. R., Rice, S. C., & Schreindorfer, L. S. (2005). Distinguishing the effects of social exclusion and low relational evaluation on reactions to interpersonal rejection. Manuscript submitted for publication.
15 Gailliot, M. T., & Baumeister, R. F. (2007). Self-esteem, belongingness, and worldview validation: Does belongingness exert a unique influence upon self-esteem? *Journal of Research in Personality*, 41(2), 327–345. https://doi:10.1016/j.jrp.2006.04.004
16 Blackhart, G. C., Nelson, B. C., Knowles, M. L., & Baumeister, R. F. (2009). Rejection elicits emotional reactions but neither causes immediate distress nor lowers self-esteem: A meta-analytic review of 192 studies on social exclusion. *Personality & Social Psychology Review*, 13, 269–309. https://doi.org/10.1177/1088868309346065
17 Levett-Jones, T., & Lathlean, J. (2009). The ascent to competence conceptual framework: An outcome of a study of belongingness. *Journal of Clinical Nursing*, 18(20), 2870–2879. https:// doi:10.1111/j.1365-2702.2008.02593.x
18 Hitlan, R. T., Cliffton, R. J., & DeSoto, M. C. (2006). Perceived exclusion in the workplace: The moderating effects of gender on work-related attitudes and sychological health. *North American Journal of Psychology*, 8, 217–236. https://doi:10.1037/e566962012-017
19 Clance, P. R. (1985). *The impostor phenomenon: Overcoming the fear that haunts your success*. Atlanta, GA: Peachtree Pub Ltd.
20 Sakulku, J. (2011). The impostor phenomenon. *The Journal of Behavioral Science*, 6(1), 75–97 https://doi.org/10.14456/ijbs.2011.6
21 Waller, L. (2020). Fostering a sense of belonging in the workplace: Enhancing well-being and a positive and coherent sense of self. In S. Dhiman (Ed.) *The Palgrave handbook of workplace well-being*. Cham: Palgrave Macmillan, 341–367.

22 Festinger, L. (1957). *A theory of cognitive dissonance.* Evanston, IL: Row & Peterson.
23 Campbell, J. D., Trapnell, P. D., Heine, S. J., Katz, I. M., Lavallee, L. F., & Lehman, D. R. (1996). Self-concept clarity: Measurement, personality correlates, and cultural boundaries. *Journal of Personality and Social Psychology,* 70, 141–156. https://doi:10.1037//0022-3514.70.1.141
24 Waller, L. (2020). Fostering a sense of belonging in the workplace: Enhancing well-being and a positive and coherent sense of self. In S. Dhiman (Ed.) *The Palgrave handbook of workplace well-being.* Cham: Palgrave Macmillan, 341–367.
25 Weeks, J. (1990). The value of difference. In J. Rutherford (Ed.) *Identity: Community, culture, difference.* London: Lawrence & Wishart, 88–100.
26 Hewlin, P. F. (2003). And the award for best actor goes to… facades of conformity in organizational settings. *Academy of Management Review,* 28(4), 633–656. https://doi:10.5465/amr.2003.10899442
27 Rogers, C. (1961). *On becoming a person – A therapist's view of psychotherapy.* London: Constable.
28 Shakespeare-Finch, J., & Daley, E. (2017). Workplace belongingness, distress, and resilience in emergency service workers. *Psychological Trauma: Theory, Research, Practice, and Policy,* 9(1), 32. https://doi:10.1037/tra0000108
29 Cockshaw, W. D., & Shochet, I. (2010). The link between belongingness and depressive symptoms: An exploration in the workplace interpersonal context. *Australian Psychologist,* 45(4), 283–289. https://doi:10.1521/jscp.2014.33.5.448
30 Weiner, B. (1985). An attributional theory of achievement motivation and emotion. *Psychological Review,* 92(4), 548–573. https://doi:10.1037//0033-295x.92.4.548
31 Lewis, H. B. (1971). *Shame and guilt in neurosis.* New York: Intentional University Press.

4
Belonging and performance – the trap of not belonging

> Another coping mechanism was that I just withdrew. I withdrew, and I, I'm the opposite of that, I am absolutely the opposite of that, but I became somebody else I absolutely wasn't in order to cope.
>
> – Delia, Business Development Manager

The key to not belonging

As we have already explored, our need to belong is a fundamental driver of how we behave. For thousands of years, we have been driven to act in ways which will enhance our chances of being included, accepted and valued. The pleasure of belonging, the pain of exclusion and the discomfort we experience when our self-esteem is undermined by a threat to our inclusion trigger us to seek out ways to belong. This makes intuitive sense – if I want to be accepted into a new team, being pleasant, helpful and interested is more likely to get me included than being distant and rude. If I want to be valued at work, I will have more chance of success by working hard, preparing well and being responsible and reliable than avoiding responsibility, doing the minimum or even being disruptive in the workplace. And this is indeed what has been found in research, where in attempting to belong and fit in workers and students get more involved in teamwork, seek out social connections, make offers of help, are respectful and work extra hard in order to be accepted.[1, 2, 3]

These types of behaviours were also found in my doctoral research – with one of the four main strategies for resolving the experience of not belonging being *seeking value* – choosing to actively engage in the workplace, throwing efforts into work, finding solutions to the experience, focusing on and recognising strength through drawing on positive feedback, successes and rebuilding self-belief.[4] Value was also achieved through establishing a sense of purpose, finding ways to contribute to teams and workplaces by crafting roles or identifying projects through which they could have a tangible impact. Elaine, for example, chose to shift her focus to ensuring she was able to establish a strong team spirit and be the best manager she could be to her team; Stuart drew on what he described as an inner strength to make an impact and make a difference in his department; and Sandra worked hard on developing relationships with colleagues, trying to identify things she had in common and build connections. These active engagement strategies work, they are helpful in establishing a sense of belonging, a sense of adding value and commonality, and we will return to them in Chapters 5 and 6 when we explore how to help others and ourselves to develop a sense of belonging at work.

Whilst a threat to belonging can encourage these positive and constructive behaviours, it often motivates us to act in ways that, whilst still designed to support our ability to belong, can in fact further undermine both our sense of belonging and our actual ability to *be* accepted. My referral to the positive behaviours as *constructive* rather than adaptive is purposeful. Just because a behaviour is adaptive does not necessarily mean that it is constructive in lifting us out of our sense of not belonging. There are, unfortunately, a few glitches in our adaptive system which can mean that our seemingly helpful behaviours can back-fire, impacting our performance in the workplace and further undermining our sense of belonging.

Trap one: ability to be ourselves

Social monitoring

One such ostensibly helpful response to not belonging is social monitoring. Our *Social Monitoring System* (SMS)[5] works by encouraging us to pay more attention and more accurately recall socially relevant information, such as voice tone, empathy or facial expressions that might indicate either that we are accepted or rejected by others. The argument holds that whereas self-esteem may act as an indicator of the extent to which we are included, the SMS is the integrative mechanism that monitors the environment, identifies socially relevant information, alerts our self-esteem and guides behaviour towards obtaining inclusion and avoiding rejection.[6] The system is considered adaptive because it encourages us to behave in ways which will maximise our acceptance and minimise our exclusion.

However, this interpersonal sensitivity can heighten our concern for feedback from others, our concern about their behaviour towards us, their comments about us and what we perceive as criticism or judgement which can make us overly sensitive to behaviours that might hint at rejection. As I have stated from the beginning of this book, our sense of not belonging is not necessarily a fact – it is our *perception* that we do not belong, and as such, a heightened concern about the behaviour of others towards us may well distort this perception. This was certainly apparent with those with whom I spoke – there was a keen concern expressed about being respected, perceived as weak or incompetent, as superior or different, which may well have distorted reality as captured by Lydia:

> I became contained, even I think my movements, you know, my physical body movements became stilted and if I said too much, I'd then worry I said too much. So, I would try, I'd really gauge, really look at people's reactions. And sometimes I got it wrong. You know, sometimes I either read someone's body language as this is someone who doesn't like me, and then withdraw. And then they'd see me as aloof and snobby. And I wasn't at all that. I think my quiet shyness comes from [being] afraid of rejection. So, I over read, I think, I over examine, and then assume, usually the worst.

Conformity

As well as potentially increasing our sensitivity to cues of rejection, social monitoring has also been found to encourage conformity, which is another seemingly adaptive response to a sense of not belonging. Conformity, behaving in ways that are considered to be socially acceptable, is driven by our need to belong and to fit in with and assimilate with others. Conformity to social norms is involved in the phenomena of bystander apathy and groupthink that we discussed in Chapter 2, it is in part responsible for participation in abominations such as the Holocaust in Nazi Germany, and corporate scandals such as suppression of the knowledge that VW were manipulating their diesel emissions for seven years. And it is a very common response to a sense of not belonging which has been found to be related to conforming to incorrect judgements by others in exclusion experiments, has led medical practitioners to become 'chameleons' and conform to established norms and practices, and nursing students to overlook nursing practices that they are not comfortable with, in essence putting their need to belong above the care of their patients.[7, 8, 9] As well as the potential ethical risks of conformity however, conformity also poses a very real threat to our ability to be ourselves, as well as to the sense of belonging that we are trying to protect.

Doctor Patricia Hewlin, Associate Professor of Organisational Behaviour at McGill University, has researched conformity for many years, and through her work developed a model of *Facades of Conformity*, touched on in the previous chapter, through which she argues that in order to fit in we *pretend* to adopt the attitudes of those around us or the values of our organisations and in so doing we suppress our own.[10] Our conformity can be expressed through adopting the behaviours of those with whom we work, expressing what we consider to be appropriate emotions or dressing in acceptable ways. Hewlin's research has found that those who work in environments which are unreceptive to diverse perspectives and values and discourage participation in decision making, who are more prone to social monitoring and are members of perceived minority status groups, including age, ethnicity, gender, beliefs and values, are more prone to facades of conformity – to behave in ways which are inconsistent with their true feelings and suppress their personal values. This in turn is related to emotional exhaustion, and ultimately intention to leave.

This is of course not to say that wearing business attire to work, refraining from foul language in the office, respecting cultural sensitivities when we work in different parts of the world is damaging – these are appropriate, respectful and sensible ways to adapt to our environments and facilitate relations and harmony. But when what we suppress are deep-rooted aspects of who we are this can undermine our sense of a coherent self-concept, and result in both the unpleasantness of cognitive dissonance and the shame of inauthenticity. This impact emerged clearly from the individuals I spoke with, with the second of the four main strategies for resolving a sense of not belonging being finding a way to fit in, to be accepted and seeking out an identity or way of behaving that would 'fit.' In talking about his experience in the Civil Service, Jason recalled behaving in particularly conforming ways, deferring to others, acquiescing to the opinions of others and not standing up for himself, with significant consequences for his sense of self. He told me:

> I make assumptions that everyone else is on this sort of inside and they are all in agreement, so that if I do try and stick up for myself it's gonna not go down very well, because everybody else's mind is made up and I am not a good enough influencer to change peoples' minds. So that's going on there…I am going to acquiesce and then feel resentful, that's a good word, about acquiescing and not saying the things that I wish I'd said and wish I'd done. Resentful is a good word because I then also resent the fact that I sometimes limit my own ability to have an impact or to get the outcomes that I want because I don't push things through hard enough.

Delia, the Business Development Manager I spoke with recalled her time at a company with a very assertive, almost aggressive culture.

> You were definitely part of the leading gang or you weren't, and part of the leading gang meant that you were strong on banter, that you went out socialised, got absolutely pissed as a fart with everybody, I mean absolutely legless. You went along with the general consensus… so I figured one way of gaining acceptance, gaining some visibility, because I was losing visibility,

> I was just shrinking away, was to meet them with that sort of bantery type of thing. But I don't do it very well, and it sort of fell flat on its face. And, because I'd tried to do it and its not part of me, that's what felt inauthentic. And also, at the pub, you know, woo, I'm having a, you know, getting really drunk, and having a lads' sort of type of time down the pub and all of that. But I forced myself to do it cos I knew I could not withdraw completely, because otherwise I'd be like a little moth in the corner and not being part of the enterprise that I was spending eight hours a day in. But I found it very difficult because it did feel unauthentic 'cos I'm just not that sort of person…it's not in the core of me to be like that, so I had to pretend to be able to mix in. And that felt inauthentic because I didn't like a lot of the banter at all, I found it really offensive I found it very hurtful, not necessarily to me, but to other people it was out of order.

The impact of conformity in both of these examples is apparent – it can limit contributions and indeed, progression which in turn will likely fuel a sense of not adding value, and as such a sense of not belonging. It can also however, undermine a sense of who we are as we behave in ways alien to ourselves, and do not speak up for what we believe in – behaviours which are unlikely to leave us with buoyant self-esteem. Furthermore, inauthenticity is essentially an inability to be who we are, which in turn is a critical factor in feeling like we belong. As such, anything that diminishes our ability to be ourselves will further undermine our sense of belonging. This is the first trap of not belonging – the way that we behave in order to belong leaves us feeling less able to be ourselves and less able to add value, and consequently we feel less that we belong.

Trap two: self-protection

Another common response to a sense of not belonging is to behave or think in ways that protect us from the threat of further rejection or protect us from the pain of feeling unaccepted. These self-protection strategies play out in withdrawal, detachment, avoidance and at times disruptive behaviour.[11]

After attempting to fit in with the banter of the office fell flat, Delia made the choice to withdraw:

> I withdrew, and I'm the opposite of that, I am absolutely the opposite of that, but I became somebody else I absolutely wasn't in order to cope. I didn't talk, I got my head down, focused on my work. Didn't look at anybody or join in with the general mood. I became far more serious than I am normally. And isolated, I think isolation is probably the most powerful word around that…But then when you withdraw you don't get noticed and you don't get acknowledged, and you don't have your ideas heard, and you lose power when you do that, that was my experience. I lost power. And I lost prominence….and actually, the result of that for the company was that

they missed out on a whole load of things that I'm really good at, that I just didn't have the confidence to show.

As Delia's experience illustrates, this self-protection strategy of withdrawal plays into the first trap of not belonging – undermining her ability to add value and so further undermining her sense of belonging. However, it also plays into trap number two: How we respond to not belonging can result in us excluding ourselves from those around us, in essence, fulfilling our own prophecy. Tragically, the self-perpetuating nature of the experience is a very common one. Elaine, for example, chose to withdraw from engaging in conversations through fear of saying something 'stupid' or giving away too much of herself, and so projected an image of disinterest and distanced herself from her colleagues. Similarly, Jason would distance himself from those who he felt were 'on the inside.'

During our conversation Stuart began to question whether his sense of not belonging too, was exacerbated by the way he responded to feeling rejected. He told me:

> I think you almost revert to an introvert state don't you. I think it's a mixture of speech, but I think it's also body presence and everything else…if I'm not getting a response from anybody even though I've tried, I might try again but if I don't get a response, I might become a bit ostracised. But, what's interesting about this whole conversation now and I'm thinking in the back of my mind as I'm talking and you're talking. I think a lot of this is self-induced as opposed to necessarily the organisation…and I don't know over the years delving into it, whether I've almost ostracised myself from getting involved or whether people have just found me a bit different and therefore not willing to get involved with me.

As I listened to my interviewees and read the various literature around this area, I became fascinated with why we make the self-defeating choices that we do, when for many of us, it is increasingly obvious that we are only serving to exacerbate the situation and bring about the very scenario we are frightened of. What I have learned is that there are two very important factors at play here: Control and sense making – our capacity to impact our sense of belonging, and the attributions we make about the role that we play in our experience.

Need for control

The former is illustrated by Clive's description of his self-defence strategies. His experience of not belonging clung tightly to his sense of not adding value or doing anything with any sense of purpose. He described to me how he disengaged almost to the point of disruption because he felt he had no way of changing his situation or having any kind of impact. He explained:

> If you rolled in at eleven-thirty you could say something like 'Oh, I have just been to see so-and-so at office X' and nobody cared if you were there or if you weren't. The only thing that was certain was the salary cheque. It was really bizarre. So, the business was not interested in you and the effect of that is, that you lose interest in the business. So, you become disengaged because you don't believe that anything you do has any impact or purpose. And you can't see where the business is going, you can't see how you can influence it and it all just becomes so negative…If I had talents, I was certainly wasting those, and I wasn't adding anything, and nobody seemed to care and so I was just thrashing about… I'd just completely disengaged – completely disengaged… I started to completely ignore deadlines, and frighteningly, nobody seemed to care. So, it had all become – it became very, I'm getting close to the plughole. I was really getting sucked into this negative position.

His description emphasises his apparent lack of agency and control, sentiments which were expressed by many others in my research. It seems therefore, that if we feel we are not able to enhance our ability to belong, the motivation that drives us may no longer be our need to belong but our need for control – if we cannot control our sense of belonging we take control of what we can – we protect ourselves through withdrawing and disengaging, and may even get a sense of control through behaving disruptively or antisocially. Indeed, research has found that a need for control in rejection experiments (where participants are ignored in a virtual ballgame) is related to antisocial behaviour, such as punishing their rejecter, or even increasing their tolerance for pain by keeping their hand in a bucket of ice![12] These effects, however, diminish when participants are presented with an opportunity to actually enhance their belonging. For example, rejected individuals in one study who believed they would be able to later interact with their rejecter were more likely to describe them as attractive and sociable and behave more favourably towards them than those without that opportunity.[13]

What I also realised from my conversations, however, was that the situations where the culture of the organisation was involved in the experience were often the ones in which the individual felt an inability to control or change their sense of belonging, and it was those situations which often led to self-defeating behaviours. Delia, for example, felt unable to change the misogynistic and aggressive culture of the firm where she worked, and so withdrew; Lydia felt unable to change the uncaring and unsupportive culture she was immersed in at the professional services firm, and also withdrew, drank more than she should at home, and ultimately left the company. Nathan was also unable to change the increasingly commercial, corporate culture of the OD team in which he worked as an HR specialist and withdrew into 'a shell' losing interest and focus on his work. As he articulated,

> If you're not happy with the role you're doing, there's potential of changing it or modifying it. But its issues with culture which I think have been the dominant ones. They're a bit different and you feel you're caught in this quagmire, and you want to, at least I have felt that I want to get out of this hole, you know, that I've got into.

As such, and as will be explored in Chapter 8, the culture of the organisation has a critical role to play in both fostering a sense of belonging and in determining the strategies employees might engage in to cope with it.

As explained, these unconstructive behaviours are self-defeating because they ultimately perpetuate our experience of a sense of not belonging, and may even at times, result in us actually *being* excluded because of the way that we behave. Work exploring the impact and outcomes of different coping strategies to all manner of events makes similar claims in that our choice of coping strategy ultimately determines our success in dealing with whatever is placing demands on us. There are many different typologies and categorisations of coping strategies, but one devised by Skinner and his colleagues in 2003 parsimoniously synthesises these hierarchies into 13 categories, which are detailed below Table 4.1.

Research has found that, similar to the active engagement strategies employed to resolve a sense of not belonging, problem-solving strategies which

Table 4.1 Drawn from comparison of multidimensional higher-order coping categories from six hierarchical systems and reviews

Higher-order family of coping	*Lower-order ways of coping*
Problem solving	Instrumental action
	Direct action
	Decision making
	Planning
Support seeking	Comfort seeking
	Help seeking
	Spiritual support
Escape	Avoidance
	Disengagement
	Denial

(*Continued*)

Higher-order family of coping	Lower-order ways of coping
Distraction	Acceptance
Cognitive restructuring	Positive thinking
	Self-encouragement
Rumination	Intrusive thoughts
	Negative thinking
	Self-blame
	Worry
Helplessness	Inaction
	Passivity
	Giving up
Social withdrawal	Self-isolation
Emotional regulation	Emotional expression
	Self-calming
Information seeking	Observation
	Monitoring
Negotiation	Offer exchange
	Compromise
	Prioritising
Opposition	Aggression
	Blame others

Skinner et al. (2003).[14]

include instrumental and direct action, decision-making and planning, tend to result in tangible solutions. Avoidance strategies, on the other hand, such as those of withdrawal or detachment employed to protect us from a sense of not belonging tend to exacerbate situations.[15] Interestingly however, the success of these strategies is also impacted by the controllability of the situation. One study which asked nurses to describe the strategies they used at work to deal with stressful situations found that whilst avoidance strategies were considered ineffective in both high-control and low-control scenarios, problem-solving strategies were only considered effective in situations in which they had high control, and otherwise resulted in frustration and perceptions of failure.[16] This further illustrates the importance of control in our ability to feel that we belong – as even active, positive, constructive approaches to dealing with a sense of not belonging will fail if we have no control over their outcomes.

Implications for performance

When I engage with leaders around sense of belonging at work, I invariably ask them to tell me how having a keen sense of belonging and a sense of not belonging makes them feel. I capture these two opposing experiences in a WordCloud and the difference between them is stark and palpable. The energy, engagement and motivation of the first scenario leaps from the screen,

Figure 4.1 How it feels to belong. Created by author.

Figure 4.2 How it feels to not belong. Created by author.

whereas the lack of energy, engagement and motivation of the second saps at your energy. An illustration of two of these sets of responses can be seen in Figures 4.1 and 4.2. The impact of both of these experiences on our engagement, motivation and performance in the workplace is apparent, and as such our ability as leaders to ensure the members of our teams have a sense of belonging is crucial to ensuring their performance.

Notes

1 Mohamed, Z., Newton, J. M., & McKenna, L. (2014). Belongingness in the workplace: A study of Malaysian nurses' experiences. *International Nursing Review*, 61(1), 124–130. https://doi:10.1111/inr.12078
2 Maner, J. K., DeWall, C. N., & Baumeister, R. F. (2007). Does social exclusion motivate interpersonal reconnection? Resolving the "porcupine problem." *Journal of Personality and Social Psychology*, 92, 42–55. https://doi:10.1037/0022-3514.92.1.42
3 Levett-Jones, T., & Lathlean, J. (2009). The ascent to competence conceptual framework: An outcome of a study of belongingness. *Journal of Clinical Nursing*, 18(20), 2870–2879. https://doi:10.1111/j.1365-2702.2008.02593.x
4 Waller, L. (2020). Fostering a sense of belonging in the workplace: Enhancing well-being and a positive and coherent sense of self. In S. Dhiman (Ed.) *The Palgrave handbook of workplace well-being*. Cham: Palgrave Macmillan, 341–367.
5 Gardner, W. L., Pickett, C. L., & Brewer, M. B. (2000). Social exclusion and selective memory: How the need to belong influences memory for social events. *Personality and Social Psychology Bulletin*, 26(4), 486–496. https://doi.org/10.1177/0146167200266007
6 Pickett, C. L., Gardner, W. L., & Knowles, M. (2004). Getting a cue: The need to belong and enhanced sensitivity to social cues. *Personality and Social Psychology Bulletin*, 30(9), 1095–1107. https://doi:10.1177/0146167203262085
7 Williams, K. D., Cheung, C. K. T., & Choi, W. (2000). CyberOstracism: Effects of being ignored over the Internet. *Journal of Personality and Social Psychology*, 79(5), 748–762. https://doi:10.1037/0022-3514.79.5.748
8 Champion, B., Ambler, N., & Keating, D. (1998). Fitting in: Becoming an insider: A nursing perspective. Unpublished manuscript.
9 Levett-Jones, T., & Lathlean, J. (2009). The ascent to competence conceptual framework: An outcome of a study of belongingness. *Journal of Clinical Nursing*, 18(20), 2870–2879. https://doi:10.1111/j.1365-2702.2008.02593.x
10 Hewlin, P. F. (2009). Wearing the cloak: Antecedents and consequences of creating facades of conformity. *Journal of Applied Psychology*, 94(3), 727–741. https://doi:10.5465/amr.2003.10899442
11 Waller, L. (2020). Fostering a sense of belonging in the workplace: Enhancing well-being and a positive and coherent sense of self. In S. Dhiman (Ed.) *The Palgrave handbook of workplace well-being*. Cham: Palgrave Macmillan, 341–367.
12 Gerber, J. P., & Wheeler, L. (2009a). On being rejected: A meta-analysis of experimental research on rejection. *Perspectives on Psychological Science*, 4, 468–488. https://doi:10.1111/j.1745-6924.2009.01158.x

13 Maner, J. K., DeWall, C. N., & Baumeister, R. F. (2007). Does social exclusion motivate interpersonal reconnection? Resolving the "porcupine problem." *Journal of Personality and Social Psychology*, 92, 42–55. https://doi:10.1037/0022-3514.92.1.42
14 Skinner, E. A., Edge, K., Altman, J., & Sherwood, H. (2003). Searching for the structure of coping: A review and critique of category systems for classifying ways of coping. *Psychological Bulletin*, 129, 216–269. https://doi.org/10.1037/0033-2909.129.2.216
15 Folkman, S., & Lazarus, R. S. (1988). Coping as a mediator of emotion. *Journal of Personality Social Psychology*, 54, 466–475. https://doi.org/10.1037/0022-3514.54.3.466
16 Bowman, G., Stern, M. (1995). Adjustment to occupational stress: The relationship of perceived control to effectiveness of coping strategies. *Journal of Counselling Psychology* [serial online], 42(3), 294–303. https://doi.org/10.1037/0022-0167.42.3.294

Part 2
Establishing a sense of belonging

5
Developing quality relationships

> I've come to a place where I understand who my really good friends are, who I can really trust. But what's really important to me in those relationships is the vulnerability, exposure, openness that we have to share mutually.
>
> – Sarah, Professor

Chapter 2 demonstrated just how important quality relationships – meaningful connections to others – are to our ability to feel we belong in the workplace. Real relationships at work not only support our primal need to affiliate with others, but they also provide an opportunity for us to be open and fully ourselves, to get support if we feel we do not belong and to learn perhaps that we are not alone in our experience.

Given we are hard-wired to establish relationships, we could be forgiven for assuming that this is an entirely natural and simple thing for us to do. However, the workplace, in particular, presents some real challenges to this, the first of which is opportunity – not all work environments, organisational and team structures are conducive to making connections, a challenge that is exacerbated by the increasingly virtual nature of our workplaces. The second is our often-natural reluctance to be as open in workplace relationships as we might be outside of work. We set ourselves 'professional' rules and boundaries which can get in the way of connecting with people at a really human level – and it is these types of relationships which allow for quality, meaningful connections and that support our sense of belonging in the workplace. This chapter, therefore, will offer some guidance for supporting the establishment of connections for those in our teams and for ourselves, and some insights as to how to make those connections meaningful.

Establishing relationships

One of the women I spoke with during my research worked as an external auditor. Elaine and her team travelled around the country spending a few weeks sometimes a couple of months in different companies. In her situation, not only was she quite literally an outsider in the organisations where she was placed, she was often an unwelcome one. So, establishing connections and relationships was particularly challenging for her. There are many scenarios such as hers, including finding oneself as a lone woman of colour in an all-white all-male team, being physically isolated at the far end of an office building with few opportunities to lay sight on another individual let alone spark up a conversation, or being part of an international virtual team, operating in entirely different time zones. Situations such as these present a very real challenge to establishing relationships and should act as red flags to us as leaders of the threat that they may present to a sense of belonging for those who find themselves in them.

Most of us, however, are part of organisations that consist of multiple departments and teams, and whilst members of intact teams work most closely together, most factions of organisations are part of a greater eco-system that functions *interdependently* rather than independently. As such, there are an enormous number of advantages to be gained from connecting outside of and across team boundaries. Identifying ways for our staff to collaborate with individuals from other parts of the organisation on projects and processes and decisions that may impact or be impacted by them, not only creates the opportunity for social connection, but is enormously valuable to the agility and creativity of an organisation – but that is for another book.

Encouraging employees to bring others into their work, asking people in other teams to be involved in what they are doing will offer the opportunity for them to make those first connections, and these connections will set off on a solid foundation. By inviting people in we are communicating that we value their input – a vital step in establishing positive relationships. Likewise offering our help, support and input to others will afford us as individuals, similar social gains. Mentoring programs are also good opportunities to establish relationships outside of an immediate team. Offering mentors, particularly to those who are new to a role or the organisation or suggesting that established employees act as a mentor to others, will present opportunities for them to develop close connections, connections which are designed to offer support but do so without the obstacle of hierarchy or power.

Encouraging connections beyond the workplace can also be an effective way to support the establishment of relationships, such as opportunities to connect informally outside of work, or getting our teams engaged in 'off-task' activities or social events to develop understanding, trust and camaraderie.[1] Working more often in virtual environments, however, can present additional obstacles here, but not ones which are insurmountable. We can invite our teams to virtual lunches, drinks and pub quizzes, encourage them to have a colleague on FaceTime or Teams connected on their desk to replicate the interactions we might engage in in the physical office and include space at the beginning of our meeting agendas for chit chat and catch up. Small steps, but with potentially significant gains.

All of the above said however, we are too aware of how easy it is to feel lonely in a crowd. The challenge of establishing connections can be present in the biggest and most close-knit of teams. We can work every day alongside 20 chatty, friendly, out-going colleagues and still not feel connected. When I was in my 20s, I was in such an environment. The world of publishing, certainly back in the 90s was fun, sociable, at times hedonistic. We worked hard but we played hard. And working in the Sales and Marketing department of an academic publishers 30 minutes down the road from where I lived offered me a plethora of opportunities to get to know my workmates well – to build really genuine, meaningful connections. But I didn't. All I could see was my difference – the one thing that put me apart from my colleagues – my lack of a university education. I could not see that most of us were in our twenties and thirties, that we loved books, that we enjoyed a good drink, that we were new to living on our own, we were bright, ambitious, and creative. All I could see was my lack of a degree, and I assumed they all saw that too. The consequence of this was that I did not join my team for lunch, passed up the weekly invitations to sit in the beautiful garden of the Boar's Head of a Friday evening, or to play softball in the summer on the common down the road. In essence, I ostracised myself and stripped away any opportunity of establishing a meaningful relationship with any of my colleagues.

So, what should I have done? As a first step I should have looked out for those commonalities – those things that connected us, that made me part of the 'in-group,' that made me one of them, instead of focusing only on that one thing that set me apart. That might have given me something to build on, a conversation to start, a relatable experience to connect through.

Second, I should have grabbed those opportunities to get to know and to be known by my colleagues. Joined them, albeit timidly, on the pub bench, taken my place as fielder on the common, and my seat in the lunchtime canteen. All of those things would have terrified me at the time – the fear of not knowing what to say, of coming across as unwitty or stupid, or of simply, as I so often told myself, of not being welcome. But how many of us would judge others for being a little quiet, for needing some time to warm up to a new social situation? We tarnish others with a very harsh brush when we make these assumptions about their opinions of us and potential behaviour towards us. So, it is important for us to challenge those assumptions, to try when we can to quiet the inner critic and negative voice, and to find the courage to step in. We will return to this in Chapter 10.

Whilst ultimately it is the individual who needs to take that step, some encouragement from leaders can support that too. Being aware as a leader of the social networks in our teams, and looking out for anyone who does not appear to be part of the 'crowd,' who rarely joins for lunch, who arrives at meetings precisely on time and disappears as soon as they end in order to avoid the agony of small talk could signal a potential outsider in the making, and be a stimulus to understanding that individual's experience and supporting them to develop the courage to step in. They may quite simply just like to keep themselves to themselves, but we will not know until we enquire.

Making relationships meaningful

Establishing connections and making those first inroads into developing a relationship is a vital, but only first step. To develop truly quality relationships, meaningful human connections, requires well-developed interpersonal skills. Not only will this allow us and our teams to be able to connect well, but it will also give us and them the tools and therefore the confidence to take those first steps. What follows, therefore, are some strategies and insights to support the interpersonal development of your teams and of yourself, and to provide a blueprint of ways of interacting and behaving that others can follow.

Knowing others

Getting below the waterline

If we are to develop quality, meaningful relationships, we need to understand more about our colleagues than just the surface-level superficial facts. To really understand Rahul who sits across the office, we need to know more than that he is 47 of Indian descent, tall, skinny, homosexual and a little bit posh. We need to understand more indeed than that he plays squash with his best friend every Thursday evening, always has his head in a book on his lunch break and gets notably agitated whenever Claire, his teammate, enters a conversation. Whilst this information may act as a good starter for conversation it tells us little about who he really is – why does he read every lunchtime, why does Claire get under his skin? If we act and judge on facts and behaviours alone, we understand very little.

The creators of the Strength Deployment Inventory®, a psychometric tool developed by Elias Hull Porter, introduced me to the model in Figure 5.1 which

Developing quality relationships 67

We see ourselves based on...   Others see us based on...

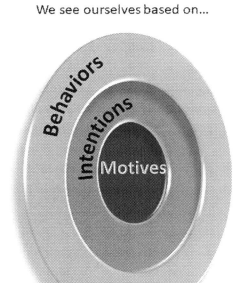
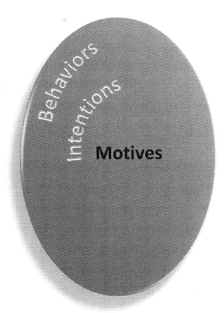

...**why** we are trying to do it   ...how they react to **what** we do

Figure 5.1 Understanding Perceptions Model, Tim Scudder (2021). Illustration re-created by author.

emphasises a very important human trait – that our perspectives of ourselves and our behaviour is based on what we know we are trying to do, our intentions, which are driven by our motivational values.[2] For example, I know that when I hold a team meeting to get input and contributions from my team on an important decision this is driven by my intention to include them all in that decision, because inclusion is an incredibly important motivational value for me. Similarly, when I ask faculty who are teaching on a programme for which I am responsible to let me have their designs and slide decks a few weeks before the programme, this is driven by my anxieties about delivering what my client needs, and if I am honest, my need for control.

However, others may not always afford us this same insight and may create their perceptions of us based simply on how we behave. As such, my team could perceive my inclusion of them in my decision-making as a lack of conviction in my own judgement. My faculty colleagues may assume that my symptoms of control are of a lack of trust in their expertise. We tend to make assumptions about the behaviour that we observe in others to inform us as to why they are doing what they are doing, and we may judge them on that behaviour.

Therefore, if we are to really understand someone at a meaningful level, to make a human connection, we need to look below the surface, below the waterline to understand their intentions, their motivations, and their values. What is driving their behaviour, what brings them to work, what makes them happy, what gets them out of bed, and puts a skip in their step on their way home? I am not advocating for an intrusion beyond personal boundaries – but simply a curiosity and enquiry beyond the behaviours we see to understand the intention and the motivations beneath and facilitate insights of them as a human being rather than simply a Project Coordinator/Sales Manager/Doctor/Teacher/Maintenance Engineer.

Lesson number one therefore, is to take a step back – try to avoid making assumptions about people based on what we see, and instead assume that what we observe is driven by positive intent, by motivations that we may well recognise, resonate with, and appreciate, if we are only able to uncover them.

Enquiry

As simple as it may first appear, there is an art to asking good questions, particularly when they are asked in order to *understand* rather than just to gain information. To understand, we need to pose open questions, questions that rather than prompt a 'yes,' 'no' response, create the space in which someone can reveal something novel, interesting or personal about themselves.

If you search the internet for 'good questions to build a relationship at work' you will come across thousands of hits with titles such as '68 good questions to ask your team-mates,' '25 open questions to build relationships in the workplace.' There are a mind-numbing number of potentially 'good' questions from which I have selected a handful that support our understanding of others without probing too deeply. These types of question might be useful for leaders to include at the beginning of team meetings, in team building exercises, or at the start of monthly meetings to create opportunities for our teams to learn more about those with whom they work. For example:

1. What would you be doing if you were not at your current job?
2. What would you most regret not having done by the end of your life?
3. What characteristic do you most admire in others?
4. Who do you consider a role model?
5. What super-power would you like to have?
6. What would a "perfect" day look like for you?[3]

Presence

But when it comes to building genuine, human connections with our colleagues ourselves a less prescriptive and structured approach is needed. Going into a conversation with a handful of good open questions will likely come across at best as clunky, and at worst as disingenuous. What really matters to building relationships in the workplace is presence, attention, and active listening. We are all guilty of disappearing inside our own heads during conversations from time to time, whether that is our mind wandering to other thoughts and concerns, formulating a response, waiting for our turn to speak or making judgements about what is being said. And I know I have been on the other side of these conversations too and observed a slight glaze to the eyes, a distracted glance to the watch, the door or the phone or an instantaneous response the moment my words have ended. And I know too that in these conversations I have not felt heard or respected and have not felt inclined to be open.

But when the opposite happens, when we are being observed with focused intensity, when we receive affirmatory nods, ah-has and the end of our sentence is met with exploratory, clarifying questions, with an echo of what has been heard or with a pause for reflection, then we feel heard, we feel respected and are more willing to be open.

Being fully present takes some practice, some self-training and some commitment, and there are many good books on mindfulness that will help you learn how to become present in relationships and in life. But for now, the considerations in Box 5.1 may support you on that path:

Box 5.1

- When your mind wanders during conversation, notice it, acknowledge it and return your attention. However often this may happen, keep repeating the same conscious, cognitive action. With practice this will become easier.

- Put aside your agenda for the conversation and be led by and respond to the human being in front of you. Where do they want to lead the conversation? What do they want to say and reveal? What is important for them right now in this moment?

- Be open and curious about what you are hearing. Reflect without judgement, even if you fundamentally disagree with their perspective. If you start with an assumption of positive intent, this will encourage you to understand more about what is informing those perspectives.

- Respond rather than react. Take a breath, take a pause and a moment to process and reflect, rather than bounding in with your first reaction to what you have heard.

- Tune in to the nuances, the subtleties of the conversation, the emotions, the intention, to really understand their experience. More on this below.

- Acknowledge their emotions. In my many years of facilitating experiential learning I have born witness to countless demonstrations of a complete, if unconscious, disregard for emotion. When faced with a weeping colleague or an angry co-worker, I have watched as others utterly ignore the tears and the shouts, remain resolutely focused on what they want to say and battle through regardless. For the most part this is not due to a lack of sensitivity, but rather a lack of understanding as to how to appropriately respond. Whilst one consequence of this behaviour is that the emotions do not get dealt with, the most critical consequence is that the individual feels that they and how they are feeling do not matter, and at best this undermines their trust in us and at worst their belief in themselves. In such situations, the simplest and most fool-proof response is acknowledgement. Acknowledge that they are upset, that they are angry, they are frustrated, they are concerned. We may not have the words or the answers to eradicate those feelings, but by acknowledging them we validate them, we validate the human being in front of us, and we start to build trust.

Active listening

Much of what I recommend above requires what Stephen Covey describes as empathetic listening – Level 5 listening. In his bestselling book *The 7 Habits of Highly Effective People*[4], the late Stephen Covey, a Professor at the University of Utah, and a prominent author, educator and speaker, outlined his Five Levels of Listening: Ignoring; pretending; selective; attentive; and empathetic (Figure 5.2).

Level 1: Ignoring is what we might find ourselves doing when our colleague returns to the office and proceeds to tell us about the conversation they had over lunch whilst we studiously stare at our laptop and punch away at our keyboard.

Developing quality relationships 71

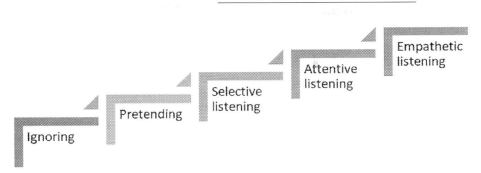

Figure 5.2 Five levels of listening, Stephen Covey.[5] Illustration by author.

It is the level of listening we might engage in as we scroll through our twitter feed whilst our daughter complains to us for the fourth time that day about the unbearable behaviour of her younger sister. In these instances, we are not even pretending to listen. Nothing about our body language, our gaze or our utterances suggests we are paying attention to what is being said. Whilst rude, it is at least honest!

Level 2: Pretending is the level of listening we might engage in with our children as they describe the new flyable-ridable pet they have earned in Roblox, the new room they have designed in Minecraft or the level they have achieved in Fortnight. It is the level of engagement we so often accuse our partners of when we are recounting the trials of our day or the woes of our friends. We, and they, nod along, make appropriate u-huh noises, but have not really heard a word.

Level 3: Selective listening is a more active form of listening. It is one which we might employ when listening to a colleague describe a new process they want to instigate. We are paying attention, but only to the parts that are valuable to us – that perhaps may support our own thoughts and provide the platform for us to jump in and agree, or that undermine our position and spur us to differ. In these communications we miss the nuances, the details and pay attention only to the gist. We have a preconception of what might be said, and we listen out only for the data that will confirm this. In this way we are prone to misinterpret, misunderstand and undervalue the other and what they are saying.

With *Level 4: Attentive* listening we are still looking for that opportunity to speak, to react to what we are hearing and we are likely formulating our response to what is being said. But, we are listening attentively to *all* that is being said. We are paying attention to the detail, to the nuances, perhaps even to the body language. This is the type of listening we may engage in when conducting an interview with a potential job candidate. We are listening to understand more about them, determine what type of individual they are, if they have the skills and characteristics to be right for the role. But we likely have the next question in our minds, are comparing them to an alternative candidate, and may be playing out in our heads how we want to respond.

Level 5: Empathetic listening is the ultimate form of active listening. When listening at this level we are genuinely open and curious as to what we are hearing. We have put aside any assumptions, biases and preconceived conclusions. We are paying attention to not just the words we are hearing, but the thinking behind those words – what does the pace, the clarity, the description tell us about what is important, about intention or motivation? What can we learn from their words, their tone and their body language about how they may be feeling, about the emotions that are triggered for them? Ultimately, we are listening to understand what they are trying to say, as well as what they are actually saying. This is the level of listening employed by coaches, counsellors, mentors, and it is the form of listening through which real insight and understanding is achieved and quality, meaningful, human connections are formed.

The final point that is important to make is to *store* what we hear and learn about someone. Remember what they tell us and follow up. I am fortunate now to have some very valuable and meaningful relationships at work. But the ones that have the most solid foundations are with colleagues who follow up with what they have heard: How was my father when I visited over the weekend, and how did I feel seeing him so poorly? Did I manage to have the burning conversation with my husband? How did my daughter get on with her first day at school? At Ashridge we refer to those individuals who ask these questions as the ordinary hero – the one that pays attention and expresses genuine interest and concern. The ordinary hero leader will communicate to their teams that they are valued, they matter, they are respected and cared about. And by demonstrating the same, the ordinary hero colleague will lay the foundations for genuine trusting relationships.

Trust

Quality, meaningful connections can only be built on a foundation of trust. If I do not trust you, I am not going to be open, to share, to reveal anything about myself beyond what you need to know as my colleague. Our relationship will remain nothing more than superficial. As such, some consideration of how we can develop that trust in relationships is important here.

I have referred a few times now to the signals that we may pick up from other people's body language. Depending on the words that it accompanies averted eye contact, for example, might signal discomfort, embarrassment, shame, guilt, shyness, distress or simply disinterest. Closed body language – crossed arms, crossed legs, a slight turn away – may signal the same. Slumping back in a chair may indicate a lack of interest whilst leaning forwards with clear steady eye contact may suggest enthusiasm, motivation, engagement and intention. I am not revealing anything ground-breaking here, these are all recognisable signals – but what is critical is both how important the unspoken is to our perception of others and the role it plays in establishing trust.

Albert Mehrabian, Professor Emeritus of Psychology at University of California, conducted a number of research studies in the 1960s, the fruit of which was his 7–38–55 Communication Model.[6] What he found was that the meaning we convey from the words that we speak is significantly less than that conveyed through our tone of voice and our body language. He found that:

- 7% of meaning is conveyed in the words that we speak.
- 38% of meaning is conveyed in the tone of our voice, the way our words are said.
- 55% of meaning is conveyed through our body language, most notably our facial expressions.

Whilst this adds further weight to the importance of paying attention to the tone and body language of others in order to determine the meaning of their words, as well as pay attention to our own, what is particularly critical to establishing quality relationships is the impact that *congruence* between these three factors has on our perceived trustworthiness. If the words that we say do not match the tone with which we say them, the expression of our face or the language of our body, we will not be believed. Our intention, our agenda, our true meaning will be under question. Imagine your boss were to say to you "I can see that something clearly has frustrated you today. Tell me what's going on. Let's see if we can fix this." Her words are spoken quickly and almost under her breath, and as she speaks, she is reclining leisurely in her chair with a broad smile fixed on her face. What would this tell you? Would you believe that she was genuinely interested and concerned or would you perhaps assume that she was saying what she thought was appropriate in this situation rather than coming from any sincere intention of support? If, on the other hand, she spoke those words whilst leaning forwards towards you, with stable eye contact and a slow and measured tone. Now what meaning might you decipher?

This example is perhaps a little extreme. But I have again been amazed by the number of people that I have observed who will try to convey a genuine message of care and concern whilst leaning back in their chairs, fidgeting, looking at their hands, and almost whispering under their breath. And it is not until this lack of congruence is pointed out by myself, my colleagues or their peers, and sometimes not until they have watched their interaction back on a video, that they are the slightest bit aware. These are bright, experienced, caring, well-meaning leaders. But they, and we in general, so easily send mixed messages through the lack of fit between what we say and how we say it. And the consequence of this is at best, we are misunderstood, and at worst, we eradicate any trust between us and others. And without this trust others will shut down, close up, and we will never be able to get beneath that waterline to understand who they really are at a human level.

So, I invite you to reflect on these key principles of developing insight of others in service of fostering quality, meaningful relationships:

- Consider the levels of listening you employ with different individuals and in different scenarios and challenge yourself to be really present, to actively, empathetically, listen to what is being conveyed.

- Practice paying attention to different levels in a conversation – to the thinking, feeling and intention behind the words, and take note of the additional insight you achieve when you do this, and the level of connection you are able to create.

- Pay attention to the way that you speak, to your tone and your body language, and note the impact this has on your ability to establish trust. And do not be put off by the impact of virtual interactions – we can still convey a congruent message through the way that we sit upright, look directly at our cameras, fill the screen and use our facial expressions.

And as leaders, I invite you to role model these skills both in order that your team and your peers feel heard and valued, but also so that through your actions and perhaps sharing of your insights from this chapter, you support the development of these vital interpersonal skills and promote your team's ability to connect at a human and meaningful level with their peers.

Knowing you

Be you

Understanding someone else is only one side of a relationship – to create those quality, meaningful connections we need to be known and understood ourselves. But if we are suffering with the insecurities of a sense of not belonging, this means we need to be brave. We need to be prepared to be our true and authentic selves. This is something which is so undermined by a sense of not belonging – as we believe that the reason we do not belong is because there is something about us that does not fit. This encourages us to behave in ways, to present a version of ourselves, that might. And the more inauthentically we behave, and the more inauthentic we feel, the less we feel we belong. So, having the courage to be our true selves in the workplace will not only support our sense of belonging but will help us to foster genuine, trusting relationships with our colleagues. There are significant implications for leaders here too in enabling this authenticity, which we will explore more in Chapter 9.

For so many years I, like many others, felt I needed to, as I described, don Miss Prim. To display a professional exterior, to say the right thing, laugh at the right moments, agree with the majority consensus and keep my real thoughts and opinions to myself. I was guarded, difficult to get to know and so struggled to really connect with my work mates. And as I rarely showed any true side of myself, I missed out on the evidence that might have demonstrated that 'I' was OK – evidence that would have come from positive interactions, trust, respect, friendship and support. But since I have had the confidence to be myself, since I have allowed myself to be open about who I am, warts and all, my focus has shifted – from myself to others, from myself to my work, from myself to my family. Being ourselves gives us the freedom to be there for others and being there for others leads to quality relationships.

So, we need to be brave and be ourselves. Recognise that as much as we appreciate and value the uniqueness of others, others will appreciate and value the uniqueness of us. So, we should be the bubbly extravert, the quiet introvert, the numbers-loving geek, the heart-led hippy. We should be distractable, disorganised, idealistic, gullible, quirky, high-maintenance, sensitive, caring, ambitious, hyperactive, passionate, funny, dark, obsessive. Be respectful, be professional, but be ourselves.

Be human

When I had my first child I, like many new mums in the UK, was part of an NCT group – a group of six mums brought together by this parenting charity to learn how to be a mum, understand what would happen in childbirth, and most importantly, support each other. This group of mothers was an incredibly valuable source of support, understanding and empathy. We shared the same life stage, anxieties and ignorance about birth and parenting. But once our new darlings had arrived, there were certain things we kept to ourselves. We talked about the challenges of sleepless nights, revolting nappies and sore breasts.

But none of us talked about the nights when we felt we just could not cope. The times we felt we were doing everything wrong, and we were never going to be a good enough mother. Not sharing made this worse for us all, because we assumed that everyone else was getting along fine and doing a fabulous job.

As I have detailed earlier in this book, every one of my interviewees from my studies told me that they assumed that they were the only one at work who felt like they did not belong. Everyone else they believed were getting on fine and fitting in, and this in and of itself exacerbated their sense of difference, of outsiderness, of perceived rejection.

You may recall from Chapter 2 my observations of two individuals on an experiential leadership development program who looked utterly out of their comfort zone – deer in headlights. You may also recall that on one of those occasions this was turned entirely around by the simple act of a peer asking if anyone else felt out of their depth. In this one statement my participant understood he was not alone. In a similar way, some of my interviewees were also able to learn that others in their teams too, believed that they did not belong; and I was eventually able to know that at least the one mum who confided in me, also felt at times, like a failure as a mother. In these, and so many other cases, being open about vulnerabilities not only has an enormously powerful and liberating effect on us and others, but it helps us to connect – helps us to see each other as similarly vulnerable human beings. My NCT confidant is the only one of those six ladies that, thirteen years on, I am still in touch with.

This is one of the things about the human race that frustrates me the most. We struggle to admit to our anxieties, to our fears and vulnerabilities, and this is particularly so in education and the workplace. We do not say to the rest of our brand-new student group when we start our undergraduate degree that we don't feel we belong, that we don't feel we are good enough. We do not confide in our peers that we feel we are an imposter as a senior leader and do not believe we deserve to be there. And so, our anxieties and insecurities continue. But if we could be open and honest, and learn as I am convinced that we would, that others feel the same, those anxieties would dissipate in an instant and our relationships with our fellow sharers would be solidified and built on a foundation of humanness.

So, it is critical that we role model this openness and vulnerability in our workplaces – share our failures, our concerns, our need for support. Demonstrate that it is OK to have insecurities, to have vulnerabilities, to have failed and to need help. Demonstrate that to connect, really connect at a human level, and develop those truly quality relationships that contribute to a sense of belonging, it is important for us to be open, honest, and human. To quote Carl

Jung: "*Learn your theories as well as you can but put them aside when you touch the miracle of the living soul.*"[7]

Notes

1. McClure, J. P., & Brown, J. M. (2008). Belonging at work. *Human Resource Development International*, 11(1), 3–17. https://doi:10.1080/13678860701782261
2. Scudder, T. (2021). *Working with SDI 2.0*. Carlsbad, CA: Core Strengths, Inc.
3. Prevost, S. (2013). *25 revealing questions that build better relationships at work*. Inc. com
4. Covey, S. R. (1989). *The 7 habits of highly effective people* (Vol. 1). New York: Simon & Schuster.
5. Covey, S. R. (1989). *The 7 habits of highly effective people* (Vol. 1). New York: Simon & Schuster.
6. Mehrabian, A. (1971). *Silent messages* 8 (152), 30. Belmont, CA: Wadsworth.
7. Jung, C. G. (1928). *Contributions to analytical psychology*. Translated by H. G. Baynes and C. F. Baynes. London: Kegan Paul, Trench, Trubner and Co., Ltd. p. 361.

6
Establishing and adding our value

> You felt you were adding value. You've got a boss that you respect, and someone that is interested in what you do, that supports you. Your opinions are valued, you're valued as a person.
>
> – Elaine, Head of Internal Audit

As discussed in Chapter 2, the second critical factor that supports our sense of belonging in the workplace is our sense of adding and being valued. Feeling that we are contributing something valuable, perhaps unique, to our teams and organisations, that we are valued for our input, for the work we do, the impact we have, the strengths we wield. In the boxed sections of this chapter I have included some tools for how you yourself can work to develop this sense of value and understand the strengths that you bring. However, there is much that leaders can do to support this journey, and that will be the focus of this chapter.

Identifying strengths

I first decided to study psychology in my twenties in a naive search for the answers to the human experience – to understand objectively, why we do what we do, think what we think and feel what we feel. But I learned, embarrassingly quickly, that there are no objective answers. There are patterns, some foundational rules, some clear adaptive drivers such as the motivations addressed in Chapter 1 – but how these manifest in our behaviour and are expressed in our thoughts is utterly subjective. We all have our own unique blend of experience, genetics, intellect, education and personality. And as frustrating as this may be to the positivist psychology researcher, it means that no one else can offer exactly what we do. We are all truly unique. One of our most important jobs as leaders, therefore, is to help our teams to realise this – to uncover their

Establishing and adding our value 79

strengths and that about them which makes them uniquely valuable, and then to help them bring those qualities into their roles.

Step One in this pursuit is to understand our teams through following the guidance in the previous chapter in regard to good enquiry and active listening in order to understand their personal drivers, motivators, values and career aspirations. Annual performance reviews of course provide one valuable opportunity for these enquiry conversations. These formal conversations however, should not focus solely on how our teams have performed over the past six or twelve months but should be used to explore their perspective on what has gone well, what they have achieved and how. What skills and strengths they have used, what has engaged and motivated them, in which areas would they like to improve? Culminating in a clear plan of action for how they can leverage their strengths and develop their skills.

But whilst performance reviews are one good opportunity to develop this insight, these conversations should not be restricted to once or twice a year. A mistake I made in my time as a leader was avoiding having monthly 1:1s with my team. My genuine rationale was that I did not want to encourage them to save up issues, thoughts, anything that they needed to speak with me about until the end of the month. I had hoped that the open and trusting environment that we had created as a team would mean they would be happy to approach me at any time. But, whilst they considered me approachable, they were also aware of how busy I was and so conversations about how they were feeling about their work and their thoughts about their development was put on hold until our bi-annual reviews. The moment I realised that this is what they were doing I revised my policy and set up monthly 1:1s. Yes, they did as I had anticipated and saved up their reflections until our conversation, but we were at least having these discussions on a regular basis.

As well as these valuable conversations, there are a myriad of tools at our disposal to help us and our teams identify their strengths. Psychometrics such as 360 feedback tools are valuable in providing triangulated and multi-perspective insights into an individual's strengths and areas for development. However, tools such as the Strength Deployment Inventory®[1] I referred to in the previous chapter, the Myers Briggs Type Indicator® (MBTI®),[2] FIRO-B®[3] and others are particularly powerful instruments because they help to develop a deeper understanding of self, values and characteristics.

There are also a huge number of free online resources for assessing strengths, values and motivators. *PositivePsychology.com* is one of many such sites that provides valuable information on a wealth of different tools, their uses and benefits, and takes, as their site name suggests, a positive and strengths-based perspective to developing self-awareness. These types of tools support us and our teams in determining what our true values are – those things that are of real importance to use – that guide our decisions and actions. Understanding what these are allows us to ensure that the work that we do aligns with these values and provides us with a sense of meaning and purpose. In Boxes 6.1–6.3 I have included three simple tools to support self-insight, which can be found at the sources quoted.

Box 6.1 You, at your best

Step 1: Find your story

Think of a specific time, recently or a while back, when you were at your very best. You may have been facing a particularly difficult situation, or you may have enhanced an already positive situation. You were expressing the qualities that make you feel the most authentic and energised. The experience made you feel proud and happy to be alive. Develop a story for that experience or for that moment in time.

Step 2: Write

Write your story as concretely as you can. Allow the facts of the story to demonstrate your strengths and values. What happened in the situation? What role did you play? What did you do that was particularly successful or useful to someone? What kind of feelings did you experience?

Step 3: Beginning, middle, end

Give the story a beginning, a middle, and try to close your story with a powerful ending. You might take the approach of reliving the positive experience in your mind, just as you were watching a movie of it. Write your story down.

Step 4: Read

After you have completed writing about your experience, go back and read your story. As you read through it, circle the words and/or phrases that you would consider to be related to your personal strengths.

Step 5: Find your strengths

Write down a list of your strengths that you identified as the result of reflecting upon a time when you were at your best.

Source: PositivePsychology.com[4]

Box 6.2 MPS process – meaning, pleasure and strengths

1. Answer the MPS questions

The first step in using the tool is to answer the three key questions:

What gives me meaning?

Values can only be a part of what you find meaningful. For instance, you might find meaning through helping others, teaching a new skill or coaching someone through a crisis. So, think back to other tasks and projects that made you feel good. What were you doing during those times? What was it about those projects that made you feel good?

What gives me pleasure?

Next, write down the things that bring you pleasure. These don't have to be work-related; you can also list hobbies, interests and anything that brings you joy or contentment. For instance, you may include reading, teaching others, travelling or meeting new people.

What are my strengths?

Last, list your strengths. This can be difficult, since many of us take our strengths for granted (they come so easily!) You might have strengths that you don't even realise are strengths, such as empathy, a positive attitude or the ability to learn things quickly.

2. Find overlap

Next, look at your answers in each area and explore elements that are common to each category, or that overlap in some way. These overlapping answers offer valuable insights into the tasks that you'll find most rewarding and engaging.

3. Shape your job or career

You can now use your answers from step 2 as a guide for shaping your current role, or to find a career that you find engaging. Put simply, you want to work on projects and tasks that, in some way, incorporate elements that overlap.

You can do this in your current role by using job-crafting (as described in this chapter). This is where you reshape your job to fit you better. For instance, are there any projects that you want to be responsible for, but aren't? Can you do your current work in a way that you'll find more engaging? Or could you do some of your boss's tasks in these areas? There are endless ways that you can reshape your role to fit you better.

You can also use your findings if you want to get a promotion, or if you're exploring possible career options.

Source: From "Happier" by Tal Ben-Shahar. © 2007 McGraw-Hill Companies, Inc.[5]

Box 6.3 Personal values assessment

Select any ten values from the list below that you think are most important to you

Accountability, Achievement, Adaptability, Ambition, Balance, Being liked, Being the best, Caring, Caution, Clarity, Coaching, Commitment, Community life, Compassion, Competence, Conflict management, Continuous learning, Control, Courage, Creativity, Dialogue, Ease with uncertainty, Efficiency, Positivity, Entrepreneurial nature, Environmental awareness, Ethics, Excellence, Fairness, Family, Finances, Forgiveness, Friendship, Future generations, Generosity, Health, Humility, Humour, Independence, Initiative, Integrity, Independence, Job security, Leadership, Listening skills, Openness, Patience, Perseverance, Personal contentment, Personal growth, Professional growth, Power, Resilience, Self-discipline, Trust, Wisdom.

What you select will help you to understand what you think is important to you and focus on aligning with those ideals in your day-to-day activities and work.

Source: PositivePsychology.com.

Leveraging strengths

Some years ago, I had a woman in my team who had wonderful people skills. She was very perceptive, compassionate, curious and supportive. She and I both recognised this in her, and during her performance review we talked about how she could put these precious skills to work. Unfortunately, however, there were no leadership opportunities for her at the time. So, we created an additional responsibility. She was to work with individuals that our Dean of Research described as 'butterflies' – those who were keen and had the potential to conduct valuable research for the school but did not have the skills or confidence to do so. My team member's role was to nurture them, help them to develop the competence and confidence they needed, help them to identify what they could bring to the work. In so doing she used her strengths, she supported her colleagues, added a much-needed additional contribution to the organisation, and at the same time developed a keen appreciation of her unique value which reinforced her sense of belonging to our team.

This is an example of what I describe as 'collaborative' job-crafting. Most definitions of job-crafting describe the art as one performed by the job holder. For example, Maria Tims and Arnold Bakker define job-crafting as "an employee-initiated approach which enables employees to shape their own work environment such that it fits their individual needs by adjusting the prevailing job demands and resources."[6] However, there are likely not a great many jobs in which employees can entirely independently re-model their roles. If Kieran in Business Development decided that updating the CRM system with client details did not play to his interpersonal strengths and stopped doing it, it would not get done, and sales would be lost. If Meeta in Product Development decided that she wanted to flex her creative skills and began editing her designer's prototypes, she would be encroaching on another's responsibilities and undermining their expertise.

Whilst as examples these are simplistic, they do demonstrate that role crafting needs to be done collaboratively – agreement and input from others in the team and from the leader of the team needs to be sought if we are to ensure that responsibilities do not get missed and toes do not get stepped on. I am not disputing that job-crafting requires proactivity on the part of the employee, but leaders do need to be involved, whether that be in green-lighting significant changes or simply being open to the idea that their employees have the autonomy to make less significant changes independently. To ensure that job-crafting supports both the needs of the individual and the needs of the business, a clear approach and strategy is helpful, and so an understanding of the job-crafting approach and its benefits for employees is valuable.

Job-crafting is typically broken down into three areas: Task crafting; relationship crafting; and cognitive crafting.[7] *Task crafting* involves changing the functional nature of the role, for example, adding new responsibilities, removing certain tasks, adjusting the amount of time that is spent on different tasks to better reflect the preferences and strengths of the individual. My team member's new responsibility of developing our 'butterflies' is a good example of task crafting. *Relationship crafting* involves reshaping and reforming the social interactions we have with others. This could involve collaborating with different individuals and teams on certain projects or regularly working alongside particular individuals to understand different perspectives and gain additional insights. *Cognitive crafting* involves changing the way we think about our work, particularly the impact of our work, to make it more meaningful and connect to our sense of purpose. The heartening story of the NASA janitor is a great example of this. The story is told that on a visit to NASA in 1962 President John F Kennedy asked a janitor what he did for NASA, to which the janitor replied, "I'm helping put a man on the moon." Helping our teams to understand the contribution of their role to the overall objective of the organisation is an enormously valuable way of helping them to find real meaning and purpose in their work and support their sense of value.

A critical underpinning requirement to all of this however, is autonomy and the control it affords. As you may recall in Chapter 4 I discussed the importance of a sense of control in our choice of strategy to resolve a sense of not belonging and ability to avoid the not belonging trap. When we feel we can positively influence our sense of belonging by connecting with people or finding ways to add value, then we are more likely to take a proactive and constructive approach to dealing with our sense of not belonging. It is when we feel that we have no sense of control over how we are feeling that we are more likely to try to fit in through conforming or behaving in ways we believe will be acceptable, or protect ourselves by withdrawing. In both instances undermining our value and sense of belonging.

It is critical therefore, particularly to our team's ability to craft their roles and support their sense of value that we offer them the autonomy to proactively make changes to their roles, to craft their jobs and help them leverage their strengths and align their work to their sense of meaning and purpose. In so doing we can also support their sense of self-esteem and self-efficacy. Autonomy signals that they are considered as trusted, competent and valued members of the team, and allowing them to increase the demands of their roles promotes a sense of achievement. Clive, my Housing Association Manager captured the impact of these sorts of practices and approaches when he told me: "*So that was a huge sea-change. From being completely ignored to being asked to prepare plans for how the business would run. I really felt that I was doing something really useful.*"

Developing strengths

As managers and leaders, we can also greatly support our team member's sense of value by helping them to *add* more value – and this requires us to be able to provide both positive and constructive feedback, offer training to develop skills and act as coach ourselves to support them in their growth and development.

Feedback

Feedback is again something which is frequently reserved for the annual performance review, for which many managers save up examples of employee's achievements and failures to be dissected in an hour and improved upon in the year ahead. However, as those of us who have children are keenly aware, feedback on poor behaviour needs to be given in the moment, when the incident is still fresh and opportunities for changing behaviour are available. Few of us would call our children aside at the end of each month and chastise them for the time that they back-chatted Nanna, threw their dinner at their sister or snapped the ariel off their brother's remote-control car in a fit of pique. The more typical and constructive approach is to challenge this behaviour when it occurs, explain why it is not appropriate and what that child should do instead. And the same approach is the most constructive approach for adults (although we may resist confiscating their stationary as a form of punishment). Feedback, both positive and constructive, needs to be delivered in the moment, when it can have an impact. We fail our teams if we rob them of the opportunity to change their behaviour and improve their skills.

There are an enormous number of different feedback models in use across organisations, however, given the importance of regular, in the moment feedback, those which are swift and simple are, to my mind, the best to use. The model I and my colleagues use most often in our development practices is the BOFF model, illustrated in Figure 6.1.

To illustrate, if a member of my team was regularly arriving late to work, I might tackle this situation by explaining that by arriving late (*behaviour*) they were missing the start of important meetings and disrespecting the punctuality of the rest of the team (*outcomes*). This is leaving me frustrated and questioning their commitment (*feelings*) and so please ensure that they arrive punctually in (*future*). The model is just as valuable for positive feedback. If a member of my team had contributed a valuable idea to a meeting, I might explain that by adding their idea to the conversation (*behaviour*) we were able to find a novel solution to our challenge (*outcome*), which made me feel relieved and positive that we would find a solution (*feeling*), so please keep speaking up and sharing your thoughts in (*future*).

86   Establishing a sense of belonging

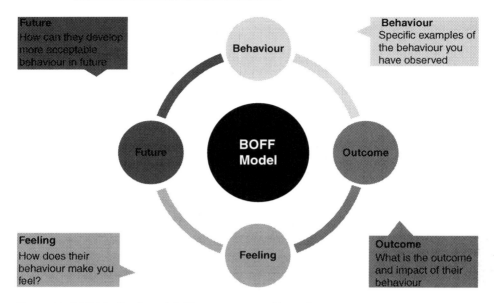

Figure 6.1 BOFF feedback model. Illustration created by author.

The value of this simple approach is that it can be delivered in the moment, through a brief meeting or, in the case of positive feedback, even via email, and so its effects are immediate. Offering feedback in a regular way also means we are unlikely to arrive at a point where we need to have a particularly difficult conversation because issues are addressed before they escalate. BOFF also involves what I consider to be a valuable combination of objective and subjective elements. Clarifying the behaviour and the outcomes, the objective facts, helps the receiver to be really clear on what they did and the impact of that. Articulating how it made us feel is a subjective experience that the individual needs to acknowledge, even if this was not their intention. Our employee would likely not have intended to make us cross, frustrated, delighted, but acknowledging that this is how we felt puts responsibility on them to adjust (or maintain) their behaviour. Finally, focusing on the future empowers those in receipt of constructive feedback to make a change and thus to improve, and those in receipt of positive feedback to further leverage their strength, supporting their sense of competence, value and self-esteem.

Coaching

Another valuable way of supporting our teams to develop their strengths and as such be able to add more value in the workplace is to coach them, that is asking questions rather than providing answers, to support them in determining for themselves how to develop, and how to unlock their potential. It is a much more impactful way to develop someone's strengths than simply offering advice because as well as helping them to learn it also *empowers* them – they are the masters of their fate, responsible for their own development. It is as such hugely supportive of someone's sense of self-efficacy and of value.

It is not however, as easy to do well as we might think. A study of over 3,000 executives conducted by Daniel Goleman, the forefather of Emotional Intelligence, found that over 24% of executives over-estimated their coaching skills when their own assessments were compared to those of others who worked with them.[8] This is something that I observe frequently in my teaching when I provide my participants with the opportunity to practice coaching one another. As clear as my instructions may be, and as positive the intentions of my students to coach and not tell, they invariably struggle to not offer advice, particularly when they have a clear idea of the solution. But in so doing they can unintentionally undermine the learning and the power of the experience.

When we help our children with their homework, we know that if we simply tell them the answers to the tricky maths problem, they will not develop the skill to work it out for themselves. We also know that the best way that we can support developing countries is not by simply giving them food, but by providing them with the means and the skills to grow it themselves. If we coach our employees, we not only support their development, but we empower them to be able to solve future challenges themselves, to apply the process of learning to other situations. The adult equivalent of showing our 'workings out.'

There are again, numerous coaching models, but the one I revert to again and again, and one that is used with great frequency across organisations is Sir John Whitmore's GROW model,[9] which provides a useful framework to structure a coaching conversation:

- **G**oal – setting clear goals for the outcome of the coaching conversation
- **R**eality – raising awareness of and clarifying the current situation and state of play
- **O**ptions – finding and exploring alternative solutions and strategies
- **W**ill – what they will do and their commitment to undertake those actions

The key to the process is asking open, exploratory questions, not simply to get information, but to allow the individual to reflect and unearth solutions for themselves. In Box 6.4 is an example of how this might play out:

Box 6.4 Example of GROW in action

Esra wants to find a way to have their ideas about a new project heard. They have identified a new process that they believe will greatly increase efficiency, but Sam, the owner of the project, whilst ostensibly listening to these ideas, never actions them. Esra approaches their line manager, Carol, for some advice, but their boss sees an opportunity for some valuable coaching. She begins by asking Esra *"What would be a good outcome from this conversation for you? What is it you'd like to achieve?"* On clarifying that Esra is hoping to determine how best to approach Sam to have their ideas actioned, Carol asks Esra to explain what they have done so far, what they have tried. Carol is also keen to know who else is involved, or could be involved, and how they see the situation. Once she has a clear understanding of the reality of the situation, Carol asks what else Esra could do. Who else might they speak with, what other approaches might they take, what have other people done in similar situations with Sam, and what have been the outcomes of those approaches? Once Esra has explored different options and possibilities, Carol asks Esra to clarify what it is they are going to do next, what they need to be able to do to take those next steps, and how committed they are to taking those next steps.

This process may not solve Esra's situation, but it will move things forward, allow Esra to take responsibility for solving the situation and help them to learn valuable skills that they can apply to other similar situations. It is an empowering experience, supporting both the development of Esra's strengths and sense of self-efficacy.

We all have gifts, fundamental strengths that make us valuable human beings. These are the things that we have always been good at, the things that underpin our skills, the things that our closest friends would describe us as being. But their value to us comes from our ability to identify and then leverage them, and our gift to those we lead is supporting them to do the same.

Notes

1 Scudder, T. (2021). *Working with SDI 2.0*. Carlsbad, CA: Core Strengths, Inc.
2 Myers, I. Briggs, McCaulley, M. H., Quenk, N. L., & Hammer, A. L. (2009). MBTI Manual: A guide to the development and use of the Myers-Briggs Type Indicator Instrument (3rd ed.). Mountain View, CA: CPP, Inc.

3 Hammer, A. L., & Schnell, E. R. (2000). *FIRO-B® technical guide*. Mountain View, CA: CPP, Inc
4 You at your best. PositivePsychology.com
5 MPS Process. *Source: From "Happier" by Tal Ben-Shahar.* © 2007 McGraw-Hill Companies, Inc.
6 Tims, M., & Bakker, A. B. (2010). Job crafting: Towards a new model of individual job redesign. *SA Journal of Industrial Psychology*, 36(2), 1–9.
7 Berg, J. M., Dutton, J. E., & Wrzesniewski, A. (2013). Job crafting and meaningful work. In B. J. Dik, Z. S. Byrne, & M. F. Steger (Eds.) *Purpose and meaning in the workplace*. American Psychological Association, 81–104. https://doi.org/10.1037/14183-005
8 Goleman, D. (2000). Leadership that gets results. HBR, March–April.
9 Whitmore, J. (2009). *Coaching for performance: GROWing human potential and purpose: The principles and practice of coaching and leadership. People skills for professionals* (4th ed.). Boston, MA: Nicholas Brealey.

7
Diversity and belonging

> Maybe being pushed out of the broader picture is the time when I have this complete, almost desolate sense of not belonging to something. That I'm being pushed out by my difference somehow.
>
> —Neil, Head of Residential Care Home

To this point, this book has focused on the sense of not belonging that arises primarily, from a *perception* of being an outsider rather from any clear and apparent act of exclusion on the part of another. Indeed, it is often the ambiguity of *perceived* not belonging that can be so damaging to one's self-concept by virtue of our willingness to assign responsibility for not belonging to ourselves, which undermines our sense of self. Whilst responsibility for intentional exclusion will more clearly lie with the perpetrator of the exclusion, actually being excluded, intentionally or otherwise by another, will still trigger the same emotional and behavioural response. It is as such, critical that we address the sense of not belonging associated with diversity, and what we can do as individuals and leaders to mitigate our contribution to or complicity in the exclusion of others.

This book was written during the year that followed George Floyd's murder at the hands of an American police officer in Minneapolis, Minnesota. That widely viewed and publicised murder threw the continued systemic racism in the USA into stark relief and triggered a tsunami of protests around the world in support of the Black Lives Matter (BLM) movement. Many nations, organisations and individuals were challenged to look at themselves and enquire as to their own potential lack of diversity, equity and inclusion and to explore the lived experience of those from ethnically diverse groups in their communities and workplaces. The serendipitous timing of the writing of this book and the relationship between diversity and belonging affords me a valuable platform to add my support to this critical and overdue shift in public thinking, by exploring

Diversity and belonging

in this chapter how we as individuals can support diversity, equitable practice, inclusion and belonging for individuals from all diverse groups.

The intention of this chapter is to raise awareness of the perpetuation and the cause of the perpetuation of bias and discrimination in our societies and workplaces, and in so doing encourage reflection on our own organisations and our own potential biases and the steps we might take to minimising them and supporting the inclusion of all members of our teams. It is not written with any sense of judgement, but to open up a space for reflection, enquiry and learning, as a first step on the road to supporting the inclusion and therefore sense of belonging of those from diverse groups.

Whilst much of this chapter will focus on race discrimination, the lessons learned in terms of the impact for those being discriminated against and the implications for how we might mitigate against discrimination can be applied to all manner of diverse groups. As such, I will begin with consideration of what they might be.

The many forms of diversity

When we think about different forms of diversity, demographic diversities most readily come to mind: Ethnicity; gender; sexual orientation; gender identity; religion; age. These are the check boxes that we most often encounter on application or data gathering forms. However, diversity takes many, many forms. Below is a list of just a handful of these, all of which can impact our self-perceptions, our perceptions of others and others' perceptions of us:

- Education – from an absence of, to outstanding achievement in academic or vocational education
- Socio-economic – such as class, poverty, wealth
- Neuro-diversity – such as Autism, ADHD, Tourette's Syndrome
- Cognitive diversity – different ways of processing information, such as introversion, patterned or visual thinkers
- Life experience – exposure to different experiences such as poverty, abuse, genocide, civil war, loss
- Background and upbringing – for example, growing up with particularly strict parents, or in an extended family household
- Geography – coming from different parts of the world or different regions of our own country

- Health – living with chronic illnesses such as Crohn's Disease, Cancer, Multiple Sclerosis, Motor Neuron Disease
- Physical and mental ability – such as spinal injuries, Muscular Dystrophy, Cerebral Palsy, blindness, deafness, learning difficulties

These are the many factors that make us who we are, that make us unique, valuable and extraordinary. However, they are also the things that can marginalise us, either because of the biases they activate in others or because of our own interpretation of these differences. As I discussed in Chapter 2, our different educational backgrounds, socio-economic statuses or upbringing may not be at all obvious or observable to anyone else in our office, but if these things are important and salient to us, then they are a significant diversity and one which can leave us feeling different, othered and with a sense of not belonging. This fact emphasises the criticality of creating an inclusive culture that becomes part of the DNA of our teams and organisations. If we are not able to be aware of the experience of diversity in our teams and the potential sense of exclusion and lack of belonging it may engender, then we need to ensure that the way in which we interact and behave is inherently inclusive. A topic we will explore in depth in Chapter 9.

Many of these diversities, however, do activate bias in others, whether consciously or unconsciously. They affect how people interact with us, their assumptions about us, the decisions they take, the choices they make. Some of these behaviours and cognitions are subtle, and as we will discuss below, may be beyond our conscious awareness. Others are more overt, more intentional, more aggressive even. In whichever way these biases are articulated and enacted, their impact is the same on the individual being 'othered'– resulting in a sense of exclusion and of not belonging.

Evidence for the continued existence of prejudice, discrimination and bias

Whilst policies, recruitment and diversity and inclusion (D&I) training now protect against blatant injustices against minority groups in most organisations, labour market statistics demonstrate that those from black and ethnic minority groups are still facing discrimination in the workplace. A survey published by the University of Manchester in 2019 found that 60% of black and minority ethnic workers had been racially harassed at work in the past five years and 60% said they had been treated unfairly because of their race.[1] An independent report conducted for the UK Government by Baroness McGregor-Smith found striking disadvantages in both access to and progression through the labour market for black and Asian citizens.[2] Minority groups were disproportionately affected by youth unemployment, with the unemployment rate of the young black group more than double that of the young white group, and ethnic minorities over-represented in low-paid and unskilled jobs.[3, 4] Research also finds that minority groups are less able to secure jobs that match their qualifications, with over 40% of all black African employees with A-level and graduate-level qualifications being overqualified for their current jobs.[5]

Evidence similarly suggests that black and ethnic minority individuals struggle to achieve the same progression opportunities as their white counterparts. Whilst one in eight of the working age population in 2015 were from a black or minority ethnic background, only one in sixteen top management positions were held by an individual from an ethnic minority.[6] Black and ethnic minorities were also less likely to be identified as 'high potential' (10% compared with 20% of White employees).[7] Those who do progress however are oftentimes left feeling like outsiders, struggling with feelings of inauthenticity, creating the facades of conformity to white norms we discussed in Chapter 4, straightening their hair, hiding their minority beliefs and their emotional responses to racism in the workplace, galvanising feelings of not belonging.[8]

These figures reveal continued racial inequalities that contradict the ostensibly improving attitudes towards race. They illustrate that whilst there are sadly large numbers of people across the world who blatantly and often proudly exercise their prejudice against people from different groups, there are an equal number of individuals who are clearly, through their words and actions, also prejudiced against certain groups but deny this to be the case. These are what Funmi Olutoye, writing in the Independent in 2020, describes as Bigfoot racists – the mythical, elusive, faceless creature of racism that few admit to being,[9] but yet reveals itself regularly, in particular, through social media.

One recent example of this in the UK was the backlash to the inclusion of the BLM fist and banner in the 2021 UK London fireworks. 2020 was the year of COVID-19, it was the year of Thursday-night clapping in thanks and support for the NHS, the year of an increased focus on the plight of our planet, and the year of the rise in BLM protests following George Floyd's murder. All these events were recognised in the fireworks on 1 January 2021. However, a loud minority across the country argued that 'political' statements such as BLM had no place in the UK's celebrations. Many of these individuals claimed that their view had nothing to do with race, and indeed many claimed to support BLM. They simply did not think it was appropriate. Whilst it could be the case that some of these individuals genuinely did not believe themselves to be prejudiced, I would argue that anyone who supported the ethical and moral message of the Black Lives Matter movement would not take issue with its inclusion in the firework display. This is, for me, an example of Bigfoot racism – racism cloaked for fear of moral judgement. And it brings me to question that if even those who are quietly racist understand it is morally wrong, why do their views persist?

Reasons for the continuation of racial inequity

Structural and systemic

Arguably the most entrenched reason for the endurance of racism and discrimination both in Europe and the USA is that they are woven into the very fabric of our nations, built on the history of our colonisation of African countries and slavery of African citizens, and perpetuated by structures, systems and institutions that privilege the white majority. Gidele Yitamben, Founder and President of The Association for Support to Women Entrepreneurs (ASAFE),[10] a non-profit NGO which promotes the development of entrepreneurship among Cameroon women argues that whilst slavery has been abolished, the system of oppression it engendered has simply been transferred to our banks, political institutions, police forces and education systems, and is continued and perpetuated by the socially constructed idea that white people are superior to people of colour.

Glenn Bracey II and Wendy Moore from Villanova University and Texas A&M University articulate how systemic racism is developed and maintained: Historically, our institutions and societies in Europe and the USA, were created by white people for white people, excluding people of colour. The exclusively white leaders and members of these societies and institutions then established the social norms, organisational structures and the criteria for belonging, for leading and for success, using their white frames of reference. These became embedded into the structure and culture of those institutions and societies, privileging whites and their interests and ultimately negatively sanctioning non-whites.[11] Historical and continued access to power therefore determines the lens and logic that is considered to be legitimate, and this transcends our societies, and results in white privilege and race discrimination.[12]

White privilege is a term that has been used across the media with abundance since George Floyd's murder, and one which again has sparked anger by those who feel an understandable lack of privilege by virtue of their gender, class, education or socio-economic status. Peggy McIntosh, American activist and Senior Research Scientist at the Wellesley Center for Women, defines white privilege as "an invisible weightless knapsack of special provisions, assurances, tools, maps, guides, codebooks, passports, visas, clothes, compass, emergency gear and blank checks."[13] It is the advantages that white people have over black, indigenous, and people of colour (BIPOC), advantages of which we are largely unaware. Whether we lack gender privilege, class privilege, education privilege, all of us who are white are holders of white privilege because the colour of our skin is not one of the things working against us.

Layla Saad, in her book *Me and My White Supremacy*, recounts her mother's words when she was a child, telling her that as a black, Muslim girl she would have to work three times as hard to get ahead, as she had those three things against her.[14] A conversation that doubtless echoes with saddening regularity throughout the households of those from black, Asian and minority groups. White privilege emerges from the historical way our institutions have been created by white people and it is maintained by the threads of legacy systemic racism in many of our societies, and the lack of awareness and often unwitting complicity in the advantages it affords, by many white people.

This institutional racism was identified in the UK through the enquiry into the conduct of the police following the murder of Stephen Lawrence, an 18-year-old black man who was killed in a racially motivated attack in Eltham, London in 1993, for which five suspects were arrested but never charged. The public enquiry into the case by Sir William MacPherson in 1999 which followed found the Metropolitan Police Service to be institutionally racist. The report defined institutional racism as:

> the collective failure of an organisation to provide an appropriate and professional service to people because of their colour, culture or ethnic origin. It can be seen or detected in processes, attitudes and behaviour which amount to discrimination through unwitting prejudice, ignorance, thoughtlessness and racist stereotyping which disadvantage minority ethnic people.

The institutional racism of the Metropolitan Police resulted in the murderers of Stephen Lawrence never being brought to justice because of the colour of Stephen's skin. Whilst many steps have been taken to address this within the Metropolitan Police, and organisations are taking steps to address this within their companies, the continued presence of systemic racism in the workplace is illustrated in the statistics quoted above.

Unconscious bias

In many instances, this prejudice arises not from conscious thought processes and intentionally exclusionary behaviour, but from unconscious bias. Unconscious biases are thoughts, opinions and assumptions of which we are unaware that are automatically activated outside of our conscious awareness and affect our decisions and behaviour.[15] They arise from our inherent and adaptive tendency to categorise, to organise the social world into groups with expected traits which helps us make sense of and navigate our way through the bombardment of information we need to process. Categorisation and quick judgements of people help us to make speedy decisions, to determine appropriate ways of behaving. These implicit associations and generalisations about others are informed by our background, our experiences and the societies in which we are socialised. As such, as the historical and systemic negative perception of BIPOC informs the socially constructed nature of our cultures and societies, it also seeps into individual thought processes, resulting in unfavourable perceptions of those from minority ethnic groups, manifesting as unconscious bias, and impacting decision-making as seen in the data.

There are a vast number of different types of biases that have been identified by researchers, but some of those that most frequently play out in the workplace are identified in Box 7.1:

Box 7.1

- **Affinity bias**: our tendency to show a preference for people who are similar to us, whether that be class, ethnicity, gender or interests, because it is essentially easier to get along with those who are like us. This bias can lead us to make favourable decisions about those who are similar to us, for example, recruiting, promoting or rewarding those who share our characteristics over those who do not.

- **Confirmation bias**: the tendency to look for evidence to support our view of someone and disregard that which does not. It is confirmation bias that encourages those with racist opinions to pay attention to the fact that a knife attacker was black, but not pay attention when a knife attacker is white.

- **Gender bias**: this can affect the assumptions we make about who might be appropriate for a promotion, for example, to a senior leadership role, or who we should hire as a secretary to the CEO. It can also manifest in stereotypes about men or women, for example, by anticipating an emotional response in women when under pressure, compared to a 'squared-shouldered' stoic response expected of a man.

- **Horn and halo affect**: are biases whereby our overall impression of someone is informed by either a negative (horn) or positive (halo) effect, at the expense of additional information that might conflict with that.

- **Contrast effect**: making judgements about people by comparing them to others rather than on their own merits.
- **Ageism bias**: our tendency to make assumptions about the skills and attributes of people based on their age, for example, assuming older generations cannot be experts in digital technologies or that younger generations cannot have the experience or resilience to lead a team.

It is these types of biases that result in the lack of opportunities afforded to BIPOC and the discrimination inherent in those statistics. When white leaders make decisions about recruitment, promotion and talent based on the extent to which the candidate is like them at the exclusion of other data, they are at risk of affinity bias, confirmation bias, the horn effect and others, biases which result in discrimination, undermining someone's sense of being valued, included, and belonging. These biases too, can result in discrimination against women, against different age groups, abilities, sexual orientations or identities, and those from 'different' backgrounds, with the same excluding effects.

Micro-aggressions and inequities

As well as impacting our thought processes, bias can also affect the way we behave, both in overt (in the case of clear discrimination) or subtle ways, the latter manifesting in *micro-aggressions* or *micro-inequities*. Micro-aggressions are defined as verbal, behavioural or environmental indignities that communicate hostile, derogatory or negative affronts or insults to an individual or group.[16] These seemingly benign acts or statements, either intentionally or unintentionally result in the target feeling 'othered,' feeling prejudiced against, and feeling excluded. For example, telling a colleague we are surprised they have a boyfriend as they do not look gay at all, may be said with the intention of demonstrating our 'acceptance' of homosexuality, but signals that somehow all homosexual men look the same. Similarly, applauding a female colleague for getting her head around some tough data may be said with the intention of congratulation, but signals a stereotype of women as being poorer at maths than men. These small, subtle and ostensibly innocuous statements can undermine our sense of being accepted, and of belonging, and given their ambiguity can leave the target questioning their interpretation, and potentially assigning responsibility for their reaction to themselves rather than the perpetrator.

Micro-inequities are another way that bias can play out in the workplace. Micro-inequities are again small and subtle events or behaviours that systematically unfairly treat individuals or groups who are perceived to be different, again leaving them feeling 'othered,' different and excluded.[17] For example, talking over a female colleague in a meeting, consistently mispronouncing the name of a colleague from an ethnic minority group, only offering childcare options to female employees.

These are just a small number of the many, many ways in which conscious or unconscious biases towards certain groups can play out in the workplace. Unfortunately for those from diverse groups, particularly BIPOC, women, older generations, LBGTQ+ and those with disabilities they are a ubiquitous part of organisational life and foster a sense of difference and a lack of belonging.

Ignorance

Another reason for the continued perpetuation of racism and discrimination in modern societies is *ignorance*, ignorance of the real lived experience of BIPOC through lack of exposure to and interaction with those from different ethnic groups, and ignorance of the continued presence of racism. Colour-blindness is one example of how ignorance about racism is perpetuated. This approach to dealing with discrimination holds that we should treat all individuals equally, without consideration of their race, culture or ethnicity.[18] Whilst this sounds positive at first glance, the approach allows us to ignore the significance of race and whiteness, ignore the presence of racism, and the lived experience of ethnic minorities, overlook their perspectives and their cultural heritage.

This is not to say that proponents of the approach are intentionally racist, or intentionally ignorant. I myself, as a naïve but well-meaning teenager, tried to convince myself I did not see colour. Ever since I was in my early-teens I was acutely aware of racism and, in particular, the injustices in South Africa under Apartheid. I had been introduced to these by the author Wilbur Smith whose books were set in South Africa and provided narratives of the story of the country from pre-Rhodes to the beginnings of the African National Congress. I joined the Anti-Apartheid Movement, I petitioned for the release of Nelson Mandela, and I watched as he was released in 1990, recording it on a VHS tape for posterity. I know with hand on heart that I am not racist, and I attempted to demonstrate this fact by claiming I did not notice the colour of someone's skin. What I meant was it did not matter to me. I did not judge people for the colour of their skin and thought as positively about those of colour as anyone else. All this was true. But in so doing I overlooked their background, their history, and invalidated their lived experience of being a person of colour in a majority white country.

Colour-blindness inadvertently perpetuates the idea that racism today is a myth, an argument which raged strongly in the UK after George Floyd's murder in the USA, with claims that we do not have racism like the USA. Examples of high-achieving black and ethnic minority individuals are raised as testament to this fact. But the same can be said of America, voting in and re-electing the first African-descended President Barack Obama in 2008 and 2012. But as George Floyd's murder in America demonstrated, the rise of one black man to the highest office in the land does not mean that racism is irradicated.[19]

Indeed, the continued presence of racism in the UK is made painfully evident every weekend with the racist tweets and stadium chants against black and ethnic football players in Championship and Premier Leagues and was brought to painful light in December 2020 in the outrage that emerged over a twitter advertising campaign by the grocery giant Sainsbury's, which featured only a black family. The advert resulted in 24,500 complaints to Ofcom, the media regulatory body, with twitter responses including *'You may as well rename yourself Blackbury's,'* '*Another reason to boycott Sainsbury's*'; and '*Never shopping at Sainsbury's again.*'

This minority public response, along with the likely thousands of daily unreported perpetuations of racism and discrimination, coupled with the statistics quoted above provides good evidence for the persistence of racism in the UK and beyond. So, why do so many continue to argue that this is not the case? Jennifer Mueller's Theory of Racial Ignorance proposes that those in power, i.e., white, suppress knowledge and nurture ignorance in order to both maintain privilege and resources for the next generations, as well as to maintain their moral identity – a 'sense of a good white self.'[20] Unawareness of continued racism, she argues, allows white people in power to perpetuate and maintain their racial dominance without *being racist*. The theory argues that we can use a variety of cognitive tactics, including avoiding conversations, paying selective attention to information, particularly that which confirms our beliefs, to sustain ignorance of racism. Because white people are those in power, Mueller argues they are in the privileged position to be able to distort, ignore and misrepresent reality despite clear evidence of ongoing racism.[21]

This continued ignorance supports what Robin DiAngelo describes as *White Fragility*, which she defines as "a state in which even a minimum amount of racial stress becomes intolerable, triggering a range of defensive moves."[22] Layla Saad argues that white fragility exists in part through a lack of exposure to and engagement in conversations about race which leaves us lacking the skills to cope with the discomfort of race conversations, as well as a lack of understanding about the existence of and complicity in white supremacy and privilege, which gets translated into a personal attack on our morality resulting in shame and defensiveness.[23] White fragility therefore perpetuates ignorance and prevents us from engaging in the conversation about race inequity in our societies and organisations.

Fear of stepping in

Fear of stepping in also presents as a barrier to change for those who legitimately declare themselves as anti-racist. Whilst many may wish to step into the conversation about race discrimination, may wish to step up as an ally to BIPOC in their organisations and societies, many fail to do so. The reasons for this apparent apathy are under growing research, which suggests that these 'bystanders' to racial inequity fail to step from inaction to action through fear of retaliation, fear of losing friends, fear of not having enough information to stand their ground, of saying the wrong thing, offending or provoking anger.[24] This fear results in a state of inaction and paralysis, leaving good intention stuck at the step before the act.

So how do we do this? How do we address discrimination in our workplaces, increase our awareness of the lived experience of those from diverse groups, and follow through on our intention to make a meaningful impact on the continued discrimination of BIPOC and other diverse groups in our organisations?

Addressing discrimination in our workplaces

Developing diverse intelligence

The first barrier to tackle is ignorance. Ignorance perpetuates the narrative that BIPOC are somehow inferior to white people or that racism does not exist and therefore need not be tackled. A recent study of workplace discrimination found that while 65% of black professionals say that black employees must work harder to advance in their careers, only 16% of white professionals agreed with the statement.[25] How to tackle ignorance is simple – acquisition of knowledge. We need to seek out, with curiosity, those who are different from us, whether that be in ethnicity, sexuality, ability, age. Simply developing relationships with those from different groups can dispel the myths and challenge stereotypes about those groups, promote understanding of their lived experience and the reality of their discrimination, promoting empathy, compassion and perhaps allyship.

Diversity and belonging

One of the concerns that so often raises its head when starting out on this path of understanding is a concern for saying the wrong thing, unwittingly causing offence and a concern about revealing uncomfortable truths about ourselves. But if we can approach these conversations with curiosity and humility, we can mitigate the discomfort. Entering relationships with an openness and honesty about our desire to learn, to understand, to share experience and thinking, and the potential for us to get it wrong. And if we do, we should name it. It will not surprise you to learn that one of the things I teach leaders is Diversity and Inclusion, and during one session I accidentally used the term 'coloured woman' rather than woman of colour. This may seem like an innocuous, nuanced difference, but I am well aware that 'coloured' bears negative associations with the language of slavery, and as such is an offensive description. My colleague pointed this out to me during a break, and whilst my stomach turned at the offence I may have caused, I felt some relief the moment I named it to the group – I admitted my mistake, acknowledged the potential impact, and apologised for my language. I was forgiven by those of colour in the group and appreciated for my candour by the white participants. Whilst this is not to say we can blunder our way through these conversations – we need to learn from our mistakes – intent does not supersede impact – humility and openness will provide the platform from which we can step in.

It is not always as easy as might be thought to make diverse connections. Living in a primarily white suburban market town in the South East of England I am acutely aware of the lack of diversity around me. Whilst I am fortunate enough to have friends and colleagues from different ethnic groups that I have met, most often in London, I supplement my lack of exposure by reading and by watching. I have any number of books on my shelves both novels and non-fiction, that immerse me in the lived experience of BIPOC. I watch some of the wonderful series that have emerged since the resurgence in BLM, such as Steve McQueen's Small Axe. I read blogs. I follow activists. I learn – the language, the terminology, the history and the reality of racial experience. I do not recount this by means of self-congratulation…these are small and simple steps available to us all. Through exposing ourselves to the reality of diverse experience we are able to challenge our and other's stereotypes, assumptions, and biases, and replace them with the truth.

Developing self-awareness

Exposing ourselves to the lived experience of those from diverse groups can shine a quite often uncomfortable light on our own biases. And this is another vital step in tackling discrimination in the workplace. Having the courage to really explore the assumptions we might make, the stereotypes we draw on, the roles and traits we automatically assign. Accepting our ownership of white privilege and our unwitting complicity in the perpetuation of discrimination – perhaps the examples of micro-aggression or micro-inequity ring unpleasant bells – explore our own inadvertent complicity, with self-compassion but with an intention to change. Expose ourselves to what my colleagues Debbie Wayth, Deepali Di'Mello and I describe as 'compassionate discomfort.' Understanding how systemic and structural racism has seeped into and hard-wired our brains does not absolve us from accountability, but it does attenuate the blame and the guilt, lessens the discomfort and releases us from paralysis.

We cannot irradicate unconscious biases – they are hard-wired into our cognitive processing – but with courageous introspection and increased awareness we can catch ourselves, remind ourselves to pay attention to all the other information we have about an individual or group before we make our judgement.

Become an ally

Developing awareness of both the reality of racism and our own inadvertent complicity in its perpetuation is the first step to allyship. Acknowledging and working to overcome our biases, recognising our privileged status in relation to others and understanding what it is that motivates us to stand up against racism will help us to develop the foundations on which to step into uncomfortable conversations about race. To challenge discrimination and inequities when we see them. These are difficult conversations, and it is not our responsibility to have the answers, but we do need to develop the competence and confidence to step in when we spot inequities.

Derald Wing Sue and colleagues from Columbia University outline a number of tactics for stepping into address micro-aggressions and inequities which they describe as *micro-interventions* – actions which communicate validation and support for the target of an aggression.[26] The first approach is to make the invisible visible. As micro-aggressions and inequities are often small and subtle, they can go unnoticed by the perpetrator. Take my example from above regarding the term 'coloured' – an approach here could simply be "are you aware of what you just said?". The second approach involves disarming the micro-aggression, challenging what was said or done and the potential for harm, such as "Let's avoid that term, it's pretty offensive." A third approach involves educating the offender, helping them to understand the assumptions, bias, historical context of what was said and the impact on others, whilst acknowledging positive intent. For example,

> I know you didn't mean to offend there, but the term 'coloured' is associated with language of the slave trade and the deep south, and so it is really quite a derogatory term to use. You should either say Black person or person of colour.

I appreciate that this is all well and good to write on these pages, and often a great deal harder to do in practice. I know this from my own experience where I have struggled and sometimes failed to step in, particularly with friends or family, when I have borne witness to micro-aggressions or even clearly racist language and attitudes. There is also the added but very real dilemma of whether the target of the aggression *wants* us to step in. If stepping in we will be seen to be taking the role of 'white saviour' – the assumption that we need to offer voice to the voiceless, and without the help of white people BIPOC will be helpless. So, we need too, to have a sense of whether our intervention is welcomed or will be another example of white people speaking over BIPOC. Again, establishing genuine and open relationships with those of colour with whom we work will support us in determining the appropriateness of our interventions.

Once we have determined whether we 'should,' stepping in with compassion and acknowledgement of the insipid nature of racism rather than with accusation, calling in (in private after the event) where possible rather than calling out (in public) can help to minimise the defensiveness and retaliation we might otherwise receive. We are all somewhere along the spectrum of awareness so our interventions should be about supporting others to move along that spectrum and take their first steps towards racial awareness and anti-racism rather than judgement.[27]

As leaders in the workplace, it is particularly incumbent on us to support others in being able to have the courage to step into the conversation and act as allies to their diverse counterparts. Providing opportunities for our teams to develop their diverse intelligence (offering them a copy of this chapter), providing training in diversity and inclusion, role-modelling allyship and creating an environment that promotes meaningful, open conversation in which people can share their thoughts, their concerns, their questions, without fear of judgement. Essentially this involves creating a culture of psychological safety, which we will turn to next.

Notes

1 Ashe, S., Borkowska, M., & Nazroo, J. (2010). Racism ruins lives: An analysis of the 2016–2017 Trade Union Congress Racism at Work Survey.
2 The McGregor-Smith Review. (2017). Race in the workplace. 2017. Retrieved from https://www.gov.uk/government/publications/race-in-the-workplace-the-mcgregor-smith-review
3 Department for Work and Pensions. (2016). 'Labour Market Status by Ethnic Group Statistics.' Retrieved from https://www.gov.uk/government/collections/labour-market-status-by-ethnicgroup-statistics
4 Department for Work and Pensions. (2016). 'Labour Market Status by Ethnic Group Statistics.' Retrieved from https://www.gov.uk/government/collections/labour-market-status-by-ethnicgroup-statistics

5 General Medical Council. (2016). 'Independent research for the GMC shows ethnicity still a factor in future doctors' prospects.' Retrieved from http://www.gmc-uk.org/news/27480.asp
6 Business in the Community. (2015). 'Race at Work 2015.' Retrieved from http://race.bitc.org.uk/system/files/research/race_equality_campaign_yougov_report_nov_2015_vfull_vfinal_e.pdf
7 Business in the Community. (2014). 'Benchmarking 2014 analysis and top ten organisations.' Retrieved from http://race.bitc.org.uk/Awards-Benchmark/Benchmark2014toptenorganisations
8 Hewlin, P. F., & Broomes, A. (2019). Authenticity in the workplace. In L. M. Roberts, A. J. Mayo, & D. A. Thomas (Eds.) *Race, work and leadership: New perspectives on the black experience*. Boston, MA: Harvard Business School Publishing Association, 135–150.
9 Olutoye, F. (2020). The outrage over Sainsbury's Christmas ad with a black family proves it: Racism in the UK never stopped. *The Independent*. https://www.independent.co.uk/voices/sainsburys-christmas-advert-black-family-racism-b1724922.html
10 Yitamben, G. (2020). Structural change must be at the heart of fighting systemic racism. *World Economic Forum*. http://dx.doi.org/10.20381/ruor-25821
11 Bracey, G. E., & Moore, W. L. (2017). "Race tests": Racial boundary maintenance in white evangelical churches. *Sociological Inquiry*, 87(2), 282–302. https://doi.org/10.1111/soin.12174
12 Bonilla-Silva, E. (2001). *White supremacy and racism in the post-civil rights era*. Boulder, CO: Lynne Rienner Publishers.
13 McIntosh, P. (1989). White privilege: Unpacking the invisible knapsack. *Peace and Freedom Magazine*, July/August, 10–12.
14 Saad, L. (2020). *Me and white supremacy: How to recognise your privilege, combat racism and change the world*. Hachette: Quercus.
15 Kahneman, D., Lovallo, D., & Sibony, O. (2011). The big idea: Before you make that big decision. *Harvard Business Review*, 89(6), 50–60.
16 Washington, E. F., Birch, A. H., & Roberts, L. M. (2020). When and how to respond to micro-aggressions. *Harvard Business Review*, July 2020.
17 Rowe, M. P. (2008). Micro-affirmations and micro-inequities. *Journal of the International Ombudsman Association*, 1(1), 1–9.
18 Bonilla-Silva, E. (2001). *White supremacy and racism in the post-civil rights era*. Boulder, CO: Lynne Rienner Publishers.
19 Avery, L. (2020). *Why systemic racism is not just an American problem*. weforum.org. agenda
20 Mueller, J. C. (2020). Racial ideology or racial ignorance? An alternative theory of racial cognition. *Sociological Theory*, 38(2), 142–169. https://doi.org/10.1177/0735275120926197
21 Mueller, J. C. (2020). Racial ideology or racial ignorance? An alternative theory of racial cognition. *Sociological Theory*, 38(2), 142–169. https://doi.org/10.1177/0735275120926197
22 DiAngelo, R. (2018). *White fragility: Why it's so hard for white people to talk about racism*. Boston, MA: Beacon Press

23 Saad, L. (2020). *Me and white supremacy: How to recognise your privilege, combat racism and change the world.* Hachette: Quercus.
24 Sue, D. W., Alsaidi, S., Awad, M. N., Glaeser, E., Calle, C. Z., & Mendez, N. (2019). Disarming racial microaggressions: Microintervention strategies for targets, White allies, and bystanders. *American Psychologist*, 74(1), 128. https://doi.org/10.1037/amp0000296
25 Bourgeois, T., & Kennedy, J.T. (2020). Steps companies can take to make the workplace better for black employees. Fortune, February 2020.
26 Sue, D. W., Alsaidi, S., Awad, M. N., Glaeser, E., Calle, C. Z., & Mendez, N. (2019). Disarming racial microaggressions: Microintervention strategies for targets, White allies, and bystanders. *American Psychologist*, 74(1), 128. https://doi.org/10.1037/amp0000296
27 Roberts, L. M., & Mayo, A. J. (2019). Toward a racially just workplace. *Harvard Business Review*. Retrieved from https://hbr. org/cover-story/2019/11/toward-a-racially-just-workplace (accessed 10 September 2020).

8
Fostering psychological safety

> I suppose it's coming across people and you know, teams of people and so on, where you talk or you can speak, and you can find things in common and develop those conversations.
>
> – Sandra, Head of Finance

So much of what has gone before in this book has demonstrated the vital importance to a sense of belonging of an environment in which employees feel safe to speak up and contribute, feel safe to ask for support when their sense of belonging is under threat, and feel safe to step into the conversation when they or others are victims of racial slurs or discrimination.

As such, this chapter will focus on this critical aspect of organisational culture, exploring what psychological safety is (and is not), how to determine the level of psychological safety in our teams and how to go about fostering a climate of psychological safety that will enable our teams to feel comfortable to speak up, to offer thoughts and contributions and perform at their best for our organisations.

What is psychological safety?

As discussed in Chapter 2, psychological safety is an organisational climate in which individuals perceive that it is safe for them to take interpersonal risks, speak up, offer their thoughts, ideas, and challenge, without fear of judgement, retribution or damaging relationships.[1] Amy Edmondson describes it as "a sense of confidence that the team will not embarrass, reject, or punish someone for speaking up."[2] In such environments it is considered the norm to ask questions, to demonstrate fallibility, to need help or ask for support. In these types of teams, we can express our diversity, reveal our vulnerabilities, make authentic and genuine connections, add value through our contributions and challenge indiscretions and inequities.

DOI: 10.4324/9781003108849-11

Psychological safety is often mistaken for trust. Trust is certainly implicit in psychological safety – it is one of its characteristics along with respect and caring for others. And whilst both trust and psychological safety involve perceptions about risk and vulnerability, trust refers to an experience between two individuals or groups – it is a dichotomous relationship – whereas psychological safety refers to a group experience, one which is typically felt similarly by all members of the team because of their shared environment.[3] Trust also focuses on the actions of others, whether we consider someone else to be trustworthy or not, whether they deserve the benefit of the doubt. It exists therefore in the mind of the beholder. Psychological safety on the other hand focuses attention on *us* – how will others respond if I speak up, will others give me the benefit of the doubt, and exists therefore in the minds of the individuals in the group.[4]

Psychological safety is also not about cohesion. Indeed, cohesive teams, teams that are very harmonious and aligned can actually undermine psychological safety because team members avoid rocking the boat and upsetting the comfortable atmosphere of agreement – as such, issues do not get addressed and things do not get said. Psychological safety is about the ability to speak frankly, with honesty and candour about disagreements, conflict or concerns, it is not about being polite.

What does psychological safety look like?

Delia, a Business Development Manager, described to me her experience of psychological safety in her current organisation. She told me:

> I would say the sense of being myself came from being able to view my ideas and have them heard and very often acted on. Being able to be as extravert as I am, and actually in that job that I did it helped, I needed to have that level of extraversion. That idiosyncrasy was not a negative. It was accepted as being quite quirky and interesting and fun…it was far more accepting of people and their personalities and their skills, abilities and so on.

Delia is describing a team that were informal and relaxed with each other. In psychologically safe teams, thoughts and questions fly spontaneously around the office and across meeting room tables. Help is sought, lack of understanding revealed, experimentation is encouraged and fruitful failure tolerated. Team members know more about each other than their roles and their career paths, they connect at a human level. They share their vulnerabilities, their concerns, voice their differences and support each other with empathy and compassion. They have a leader who is transparent, approachable and humble.[5]

The extreme antithesis of these types of teams, teams who *lack* psychological safety are often more reserved and formal. Team members stick to their specific responsibilities, keep their concerns and questions to themselves, rarely admit to not-knowing and contribute little to discussions through fear of being wrong or being judged. Relationships are likely to be surface level, and outside work connections few and far between. Team members may be solitary creatures, arriving on the dot for meetings and leaving the moment they are over, with heads bent over devices to avoid eye contact and chit chat. These kinds of unsafe team often exhibit emotional conflict, as challenge of perspectives or questioning of ideas is perceived as threatening, leading to defensive behaviour. Individuals are also often quite controlling, particularly over their area of expertise, as a lack of safety motivates a drive for control and security. Leaders are typically distant and authoritative.

These are two extremes of a continuum but illustrate the impact of the presence or absence of psychological safety on our ability to speak up, add value, get support, or challenge, and feel like we belong.

If you reflect on the behaviours and atmosphere in your own team, you may be able to gauge whether it is a psychologically safe environment or not. There are, however, a number of tools available to help you assess this more objectively. Box 8.1 contains a survey created by Amy Edmondson which has been used in countless research studies and by many organisations. My invitation to you is to try this out with your team. The higher the score the

---

Box 8.1 Survey measure of psychological safety, Amy Edmondson (1999)[6]

1   If you make a mistake in this team, it is often held against you.

2   Members of this team are able to bring up problems and tough issues.

3   People in this team sometimes reject others for being different.

4   It is safe to take a risk in this team.

5   It is difficult to ask other members of this team for help.

6   No-one in this team would deliberately act in a way that undermines my efforts.

7   Working with members of this team, my unique skills and talents are valued and utilised.

Note: The questions need to be ranked from 1–7 or 1–5 on a scale from strongly agree (5 or 7) to strongly disagree (1). Questions 1, 3 and 5 need to be scored in reverse (1 = strongly agree).

higher the level of psychological safety in your team. You can also use the average scores across individual questions to explore certain areas in more depth, asking for examples of positive and poor behaviour to identify some tangible areas for change.

Fostering psychological safety

Leader characteristics

As leaders we have a vital role to play in establishing a climate of psychological safety in our teams. The way that we lead both sets the standard and expectation for how we want others to behave in our teams, as well as determines whether relationships and people are prioritised alongside task and process. A relational approach to leadership will prioritise people and relationships and the connections and interactions with our team and within our team, and this in turn will support the development of the quality relationships discussed in previous chapters.

A key attribute of leaders who foster psychological safety is *authenticity*. Leaders who deliver on their promises, represent and support the interests of their teams no matter the potential cost to themselves. When they ask for input, these leaders act on it rather than pay lip service to it. There is little more demoralising than being asked for your input on a new process, decision or strategy on the basis of a consultative approach to decision-making, only to find a notable absence of any of the discussions and contributions that were made in the final decision. Not only is this a disheartening waste of time and effort, but it seriously undermines trust in the organisation's leadership and signals a lack of trust in and value of employee's perspectives. Authentic leaders, however, listen to the input they hear, reflect on it, enquire around it, build on it, and integrate it genuinely into their plans and decisions. This signals that team members are trusted, valued and valuable.

Being *humble*, aware of our personal limitations and weaknesses, open about what we do and do not know, and about our concerns and anxieties is also critical to the development of psychological safety, as it demonstrates that it is okay to not have all the answers and signals our need for our team's input. However, as leaders, talking openly about our vulnerabilities and failures can be particularly challenging. We often believe that in order to demonstrate credibility and ensure other's confidence in us and our ability to lead, we need to be fool-proof, we need to always be seen to get things right and to have all the answers. But never getting things wrong, never admitting to when things go wrong, or an over reliance on our own expertise and credibility as a leader can be received by our teams as intimidating. It emphasises our status as leader, and the power differential between us, it sends the message to our teams that we do not need to hear their input, and thus diminishes their courage to offer their thoughts.

In *The Fearless Organisation* Amy Edmondson describes the antithesis of foolproof leaders as 'don't knowers.'[7] She discusses Eileen Fisher, founder of the clothing brand of the same name, who role modelled humility and vulnerability, being open about what she did not know, when she needed help, and about her fears and struggles as a leader. This allowed others in the organisation to feel safe enough to offer their help and fill in the gaps in her knowledge as well as be open about their own concerns. It also conveyed the message that having their own fears and anxieties about their role, their responsibilities or the future stages of their career did not mean they were not up to the job and did not mean they did not have the courage to be a leader. Humility *requires* courage, courage to ask for candid feedback and courage to admit to our vulnerabilities. Good leaders are humble.

This type of leader was exemplified in a Head of HR that I encountered whilst working with a healthcare organisation. During the leadership development programme, the Head of HR was generous enough to talk to the group about her leadership journey. During this session she described, with openness and honesty, both her achievements and challenges as a leader. She talked about her feelings of imposter syndrome as she stepped into one organisation, feeling out of her depth and on her own. She described the struggle she had with a conflict of values on another step on her journey, and about her reluctance but eventual acceptance that she needed to walk away. She talked about her concerns as a working mother, balancing raising her daughter and managing her career, and her concerns about the impact of this on her opportunities and progression. Her openness, integrity and humility set the stage of expectation – senior leaders in the organisation have their fears – it is okay if you do too.

Interpersonal skills

The interpersonal skills of the leader of a psychologically safe team reflect those I explored in Chapter 5 – presence, active listening, focused attention and empathy. These skills allow us to understand our teams, to understand what is important to them, what motivates them, what their concerns and fears might be. Empathy allows us to see things from their perspective, to walk in their shoes, and provides us with the insight to be respectful and sensitive in the way that we interact. The leader who talks over their team in meetings, is constantly distracted by their phone, watch or the door, who criticises them in front of their peers or dismisses their concerns will eradicate any chance that their teams will feel safe to speak up and be heard. But the leader who demonstrates they are paying attention by summarising what they hear, checking their understanding, offering affirmative nods ensures their team feel understood, supported and cared for. This encourages them to be themselves, to be open, honest, speak up and take risks. As such, paying attention to and practicing with those skills from Chapter 5 will also support us in fostering psychological safety in our teams.

Permission to care

The CEO of the same company as the Head of HR I talked of above demonstrated through his leadership the values of compassion, caring, respect, loyalty and integrity. He wove these values throughout the organisation through the principles he established, modelled and lived. He was a glowing example to leaders and potential leaders of the organisation that making it to the top can be achieved through compassion and caring as well as results and performance. Through the way that he led the company he gave his leaders and his employees permission to care for each other.

Whilst this might appear to be an unnecessary emphasis, one of the things I have learned through my research and years of practice is that we so easily as leaders, faculty, employees undervalue compassion, caring and the human connection. When I first stepped into a senior leadership position I, like so many, was concerned as to whether I had what it took to lead. I knew I had to leave behind the technical expertise that had got me to that position and to work out who I was as a leader – how I would influence those below and above me, how I would motivate my team and my peers. In the end I went with my instincts, in a rather unplanned and impulsive way. I was not aware at the time of how I was leading, but on reflection I led with my heart. My focus was on how my team experienced the workplace – whether they felt valued, trusted, cared for, included, supported. Their well-being was subconsciously the top of my to-do list. I was concerned that my bosses believed I could not deliver results without an authoritative approach to leading, and that I would discover that they were right. My team may like me, but would they respect me? However, the impact of my leadership approach was that they bent over backwards to deliver, to add value, to achieve. They wanted to do well for both themselves and for me. I was not aware of what I was doing at the time, but I was establishing a climate of psychological safety through caring for my team, by making them feel that they mattered and were valued.

It was not until I was faced with my next transition into faculty and began to again worry about what I would bring to that role that my coach helped me to identify it – my warmth, my compassion, and my genuine concern for others.

That was why my team experienced me the way they did, that was why they performed the way they did, and why I surprised myself at being good at leading. And it was that which I would bring into the classroom and to my relationships with my clients and my students. My coach helped me to see the value of my compassion and in so doing gave me permission to care.

My under-valuing of compassion is not uncommon. I have heard so many around me similarly undervalue the power and impact of their compassionate approach. A recent conversation with an executive coach revealed she was struggling with what she considered the polarity between her natural relational approach to coaching and the need to 'sell' her 'product' to corporations. She struggled to appreciate that her 'product' *was* her relational approach, her compassion and her warmth, and that that was all she needed to 'sell' in order to keep a roof over her and her son's heads.

Tolerance of failure

One of the critical barriers to those in our teams feeling comfortable speaking up, contributing and taking interpersonal risks is a fear of failure. This is of course, an entirely natural phenomenon. But when we take risks, push boundaries and experiment, things do go wrong. But when failure is received with blame, judgement and punishment, no-one takes risks, no-one experiments and pushes boundaries and no-one steps up. Conversely, receiving failure with empathy, curiosity and a growth mindset focused on understanding the factors and improving for the future, fosters psychological safety, encourages experimentation, risk taking, innovation and speaking up.[8] A tolerant approach to failure can be communicated by the vulnerability and humility we model as leaders as discussed above, as well as through the language we use when we talk about failures. When we refer to them as mistakes, as poor decisions or errors of judgement, we confer blame. But reframing failures as experiments that did not work, as challenges to be overcome, and demonstrating gratitude for the process, for the quality of the work and the collective efforts, extinguishes blame and recognises the positive intent and the courage to take the risk. Talking about what can be learned, what we can try differently, what might work better in the future, sets failure up as an opportunity for learning rather than a cause for chastisement.

In essence, we need to not focus on getting it right, on the success of the end result, but recognise and reward the process and the journey, the collaboration, the innovation, the creativity, the relationships, the bravery and the hard work. Then our teams will feel safe to speak up and take a risk.

Addressing the unspoken

What we are trying to establish is an environment in which all of our teams have the courage to find their voice and speak up not just about their ideas and contributions, but also about their fears, concerns and inequities. The latter requires real courage on the part of our teams and a clear demonstration of our intent as leaders. In my research for this book, I came across a blog from a company called Fearless Culture, entitled 'Uncover the Stinky Fish.' It promotes the facilitation of workplace conversations around concerns and anxieties through the use of four questions set out on a 2 × 2 matrix (see Figure 8.1). This matrix can be completed one per team member or one for the whole team, with individuals asked to add their responses to the questions on a sticky note. These are then compared for commonalities, contradictions and tensions, themes identified and prioritised for addressing by the team. This is a simple but effective way of bringing silent problems into the open to be discussed and explored by the whole team, whilst signalling genuine intent to create a speak up culture.

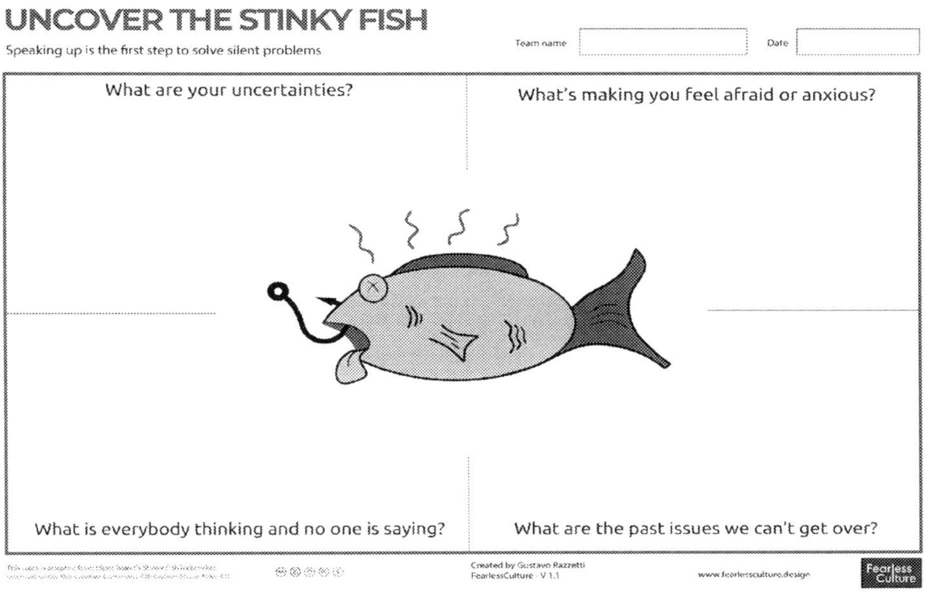

Figure 8.1 The Uncover the Stinky Fish Canvas © 2019–2021 was created by Gustavo Razzetti, Fearless Culture, and licensed by CreativeCommons. It was inspired by an activity by HyperIsland. Illustration by Tristán Razzetti.[9]

Inclusive leadership

The final vital ingredient to fostering psychological safety is inclusive leadership. As I have touched on already in this chapter, inviting, recognising and acting on contributions from our teams and meeting them with curiosity and respect sends a clear signal both of our desire for them to speak up, but also our fallibility, and their worth. Given the fundamental value of inclusive leadership to directly supporting an individual's sense of belonging as well as its value in fostering psychological safety, we shall explore this in the following chapter.

Notes

1 Edmondson, A. C. (1999). Psychological safety and learning behavior in work teams. *Administration Science Quarterly*, 44(2), 350–383. https://doi.org/10.2307/2666999
2 Edmondson, A. C. (1999). Psychological safety and learning behavior in work teams. *Administration Science Quarterly*, 44(2), 350–383, p. 354 https://doi.org/10.2307/2666999
3 Edmondson, A. C. (2003). Speaking up in the operating room: How team leaders promote learning in interdisciplinary action teams. *Journal of Management Studies*, 40, 1419–1452. https://doi.org/10.1111/1467-6486.00386
4 Edmondson, A. C. (2019). *The fearless organization: Creating psychological safety in the workplace for learning, innovation and growth*. Hoboken, NJ: John Wiley & Sons.
5 Edmondson, A. C. (2019). *The fearless organization: Creating psychological safety in the workplace for learning, innovation and growth*. Hoboken, NJ: John Wiley & Sons.
6 Edmondson, A. C. (1999). Psychological safety and learning behavior in work teams. *Administration Science Quarterly*, 44(2), 350–383.
7 Edmondson, A. C. (2019). *The fearless organization: Creating psychological safety in the workplace for learning, innovation and growth*. Hoboken, NJ: John Wiley & Sons.
8 Dweck, C. (2015). Carol Dweck revisits the growth mindset. *Education Week*, 35(5), 20–24.
9 Razetti, G. (2019). Uncover the stinky fish canvas. https://www.fearlessculture.design/blog-posts/uncover-the-stinky-fish-canvas

9
Being an inclusive leader

> The ambiance was entirely different you know, far more accepting of people and their personalities and their, you know, difference, skills, abilities and so on. So, I felt very much myself there.
>
> – Delia, Business Development Manager

In Chapter 7, I talked about the importance of addressing discrimination, inequity and exclusion of those from diverse groups in our workplaces. In the previous chapter, I discussed the importance of creating a space of psychological safety in order for everyone in our teams and organisations to find their voice, have that voice heard and be included in the discussion. Critical to both of these fundamentals is inclusion. Throwing together a healthy heterogenous mix of individuals will not, by itself, result in them feeling included and experiencing a sense of belonging (or indeed help us to reap the enormous organisational benefits of a diverse workforce). And creating an environment in which all feel safe and comfortable to speak up is an entirely academic pursuit if they are not invited to offer their voice for inclusion in the conversation.

My colleague Debbie Wayth describes diversity as the *fact* – the makeup of your workforce – and inclusion as the *act* – the behaviours that ensure that those from diverse groups feel included and able to establish a sense of belonging. It is as such possibly the most foundational leadership ingredient to supporting a sense of belonging in the workplace.

So, what do we mean by inclusive leadership? There are many definitions of the inclusive leader, but the one that captures it most appropriately for me is that which is at the heart of the Inclusive Leadership Approach (ILA) developed through an EU funded partnership designed to support practitioners who work alongside those at risk of exclusion from society. They describe an inclusive leader as:

> Having the courage to take conscious steps to break down barriers for people at risk of being excluded from society. Inclusive leaders embody a leadership

DOI: 10.4324/9781003108849-12

approach that appreciates diversity, invites, and welcomes everyone's individual contribution, and encourages full engagement with the processes of decision-making and shaping reality. The aim of inclusive leadership is to create, change and innovate whilst balancing everybody's needs.[1]

This description captures three key components of inclusive leadership: An open, fair and curious mindset; collaborative behaviours to bring all into the conversation; and the courage and commitment to stand true to beliefs in support of an inclusive organisation.

An inclusive mindset

First and foremost, an inclusive leader approaches leadership with *humanity, compassion and respect*, what the ILA refers to as an approach based on human rights and an acknowledgement of everybody's inherent worth. Inclusive leaders underpin their leadership practice with values of equality, equity and fairness. They personalise individuals by recognising and appreciating their unique values and identities, strengths, characteristics, background and experience rather than drawing on stereotypes and assumptions.[2] An inclusive leader will start with an assumption of positive intent, that their team members are driven to show up, try hard and add value. If a member of their team is quiet in team meetings an inclusive leader will first assume that they are paying attention, listening intently and internally processing what they are hearing, rather than assume that they are distracted and disengaged. In so doing they accept their team members for all that they are, without judgement. This mindset allows their teams to be their authentic selves in the workplace, supporting their sense of value and belonging.[3]

The inclusive leader also has an *open* and *curious mind*. They are genuinely interested in hearing the opinions of others, understanding their experience and perspective and learning something novel and potentially contradictory to their own opinion. They are accepting of paradox and ambiguity, and the ubiquitous presence of uncertainty. Accompanying this is the courage to suspend and the humility to let go of their beliefs and perspectives in the face of alternatives, accepting when they are wrong, have overlooked something critical, made assumptions or leapt to conclusions.[4]

Critical to this is the *self-awareness, humility* and *vulnerability* that I discussed in previous chapters – an awareness of the assumptions we may make, the stereotypes we draw on, the conscious or unconscious biases we may hold, and the commitment to notice and challenge them and their influence on our thinking and decision-making. Awareness and then acceptance of who we are, our blind-spots, limitations and fears pave the way for acceptance of those of others. It also enables us to be our authentic selves in the workplace – strengths, values, failures, warts and all. It allows us to be transparent about our concerns, our views and our motivations and role model to others our appreciation and encouragement of their own true authenticity.

According to Deloitte's model of inclusive leadership, the inclusive leader mindset is culturally intelligent, aware of both the different perspectives, values and norms of different cultural groups.[5] They have an insight into cultural dynamics, tensions and misunderstandings that might arise in their teams, across departments or the broader business, and are able to adjust their interactions, their language and their behaviour to respect those differences and minimise conflict. They are also aware of the cultural lens through which they view the world, the filter of privilege, bias or preference that influences their view of reality. They appreciate the value and unique understanding of the world brought by different cultures and are open to question their own culturally determined view.[6]

This openness can present some significant challenges, particularly when deeply held values are involved. A student on one of my D&I workshops recounted to me an incident whereby the father of a potential student from the Middle East refused to speak with her about his son's enrolment as he wanted to speak to a man. In that situation, there was an enormous tension for my student between respecting the perspective and values of the caller and being true to her own value of gender equality. In the end, she politely explained to him that she did not hold his view and she was confident that she would be able to deal with his requests, but in respect of his beliefs she would pass him over to a male colleague if that was his preference. In the end, he decided to decline her offer, spoke with the female enrolment officer and his son began a fruitful master's degree at the university.

Inclusive behaviours

So, what does this mean in practice? What should we be doing in order to ensure we are leading and behaving inclusively in the workplace?

Collaboration

To translate this open, respectful and curious mindset into practice requires a willingness to collaborate in our decision-making and to give away some of our power and leadership to those in our teams. Otto Sharmer, a senior lecturer at MIT suggests:

> You lead by painting a picture that is intentionally incomplete; you make a few strokes; and you leave lots of blank space that others can add to and participate in. By operating this way, you shift the power dynamics from ownership to belonging.[7]

By leaving gaps in our thinking, we create the space into which our teams can step, contributing their ideas and adding value. Inclusive leadership involves behaviours which deliberately and proactively invite team members into discussions and decisions, as well as appreciative behaviours, such as a positive response to contributions that demonstrates those perspectives are valued.

I recall a comment from a participant on a programme I was running some years ago. When discussing the importance of collaboration and inclusion in decision-making, he stated 'But not everyone's ideas are useful. Not everyone knows what they are talking about!.' I shared with him the approach to decision-making taken by a colleague of mine. Before offering his own perspective, he would ask his team to offer theirs and listen with the intention of understanding why their perspective may be different to his, what insights they were bringing to the discussion that he had not considered, analysing and questioning his own opinion. He told me that invariably one of two things would happen – the team would either arrive together at the same, albeit fully fleshed out decision that he had already contemplated, or they would arrive at a completely different, but considerably better position on the matter. Either way, not only was the outcome significantly smarter, but each voice felt, and was, heard, valued and respected. Those with less experience learned an enormous amount from the process, and the team as a whole felt empowered, and the decision owned.

Sarah, the leadership development consultant I spoke with during my research, shared with me her experience of finally finding an organisation that treated her inclusively, and allowed her to speak up and value what she brought.

> The stuff I love about [company] is the variety we are able to do and the empowerment with which we're able to do it. And the lovely trust we have with one another about how and when we accomplish it… And I think as you get older you understand the greatness of being different, and the difficulty of being different…If you're different, good. I'm different in that I bring great skills to this organisation you've not had before. I have said things that have made you think and not shut down.

Reaping the benefits of including diverse perspectives involves what Roger Martin, Academic Director of the Martin Prosperity Institute at the Rotman School, describes as integrative thinking. It involves:

> the ability to face constructively the tension of opposing ideas and, instead of choosing one at the expense of the other, generate a creative resolution of the tension in the form of a new idea that contains elements of the opposing ideas but is superior to each.[8]

Integrative thinking is key to inclusive leadership, a journey which, according to my colleagues Sharon Olivier and Frederick Hölscher involves four steps: exclude; tolerate; accommodate; and innovate.

Excluding involves actively not listening, ignoring or silencing others. *Tolerating* involves the recognition of difference and different perspectives and an acceptance that for the sake of political correctness and harmony we need to pay attention, be respectful and friendly. *Accommodating* involves actively listening, with curiosity to others' perspectives, and then compromising our own views to accommodate those of others. There is, however, a limit to which we will go to include those perspectives in our decision-making. The fourth level, *innovating*, involves the integration of different perspectives to arrive at something new – the power of 1 + 1 = 3. It requires an openness to re-spect, re-look and understand the value of different insights and perspectives.[9]

Integrative thinking requires the capacity to manage polarities, polarised viewpoints, by identifying the upsides and downsides of different perspectives, and coming to a solution that maximises the benefits of both and minimises the limitations of both.[10] For example, a recognisable polarity in many teams may be between control and autonomy. The potential up and downsides of both are captured in the matrix in Table 9.1. Integrative thinking would seek a solution to this polarity that ensured consistency and efficiency were maintained and risks minimised, whilst supporting creativity, innovation, and empowering teams. That might involve, for example, allowing autonomy in the process of

Table 9.1 Polarity map of control vs. autonomy, based on Olivier, Hölscher and Williams[11]

	Control	*Autonomy*
Upsides	Ordered	Empowerment
	Systematic	Creativity
	Consistency	Innovation
	Efficiency	Efficiency
	Low risk	Commitment
		Engagement
Downsides	Low creativity	Lack of coordination
	Disengagement	Inconsistency
	Disempowerment	Lack of speed
	Demotivated	Risk of mistakes
	Over-worked management	Lack of clarity over responsibility
		Poor decision-making

achieving an agreed outcome, or flexibility in how to meet a goal within certain boundaries.

An understanding of how to identify and map these polarities allows us to reap the rewards of inclusive leadership and as such encourages its proliferation.

Inclusive conversations

The ability to collaborate and hold inclusive conversations requires the interpersonal skills of attention, active listening, open questions, trust, and rapport that I discussed in Chapter 5. It also necessitates the psychological safety that I discussed in the previous chapter, ensuring an environment in which everyone feels comfortable to offer their thoughts and ideas irrespective of level, role, or experience. As a leader it is incumbent on us to role model respect, acceptance and openness in our teams, and to establish a group identity to ensure the team recognise the value of everyone's contribution to the goals of the group. It is also important that we contract with our teams around the ways in which we will work together in team meetings, for example, not interrupting or talking over others, allowing space for others to step in, and intervening to change unhelpful patterns of communication.

It is also critical that we invite contributions in a way that suits different people's preferences for contributing. A member of one of the teams I used to lead was what I (and he) described as 'screamingly introverted'. He was incredibly bright, had really insightful and very often diverse perspectives to offer, but found it a huge challenge to offer those thoughts in our meetings. We discussed this, between the two of us, regularly. I wanted to find a way to bring him in without putting him on the spot. We agreed that if he did not spontaneously offer his thoughts, I would ask him if he had anything to add. If he did and just could not find the space to speak, he would be able to step into that space. If he were still processing, which, as an introvert was often the case, he would say so and that he would follow up with me later. This worked for him, and meant the team reaped the benefits of his hugely valuable insights and he felt empowered, valuable, and not judged for being a 'silent type'. Others, however, might need a different approach, the space perhaps to speak one to one, or the opportunity to offer their voice via email. However we receive these contributions, it is vital that we clarify that they are as valued, considered and incorporated as others.

PositivePsychology.com suggest an approach to inclusive conversations called 1-2-4-All, whereby team members are encouraged to contribute by first working on their own, then in pairs, then fours, and then in the whole group.[12] Individuals first work on their own to explore an idea and clarify their thinking on a matter. They are then paired up to share their ideas and next asked to reflect on similarities and contradictions between them, and to build on each other's ideas. These pairs then pair up with another pair to form a foursome to continue building, before the key thoughts are shared with the whole group. This way thoughts can be formulated individually, tested out with just one other, before being built on and incorporated into the co-created decision.

As a leader it is also important that we ourselves, reflect on the quality of the conversations within our teams and consider, for example:

- Do we give equal time to all members of our team, or favour those who think like us or are more likely to agree with us?
- Do we give more time and attention to those who are located in our building over those who join meetings virtually?
- Are there any patterns of behaviour that prevent good conversations from happening?
- What things are not discussed in our team and why is it they cannot be discussed?

Courage and commitment

True inclusive leadership also requires courage, courage at a number of levels. First, it takes courage for a leader to disperse some of their power to their teams in order to include them in their decisions. Relinquishing some of the power that comes with leadership, has no doubt been worked hard for, takes bravery and self-assurance. It also takes courage to trust those in your team to deliver on your behalf without your interference and requires a level of comfort with risk and tolerance of intelligent failure. And as research suggests that the disruption and potential conflict that can occur in the early stages of the development of diverse teams means they are actually outperformed by homogenous teams, inclusive leadership requires the courage and emotional resilience to stay the course and trust the process.[13] It also takes courage for leaders to be open to new ways of thinking and to explore new paths and solutions, to present these to their superiors, and to be prepared to respond to the challenge, resistance and push back they may get from different levels in the organisation.

Inclusive leadership also requires the courage to speak up, for both ourselves and for others. Deloitte propose that speaking up and challenging happens at three levels: With others; with the system; and with ourselves. *Challenging others* might involve the allyship we discussed in Chapter 7, challenging discriminatory behaviour, unhelpful ways of communicating, disrespectful ways of interacting, by calling in or calling out – helping others to understand the impact of their behaviour on other people as well as the performance of the team. *Challenging the system* takes this to the level of the systemic institutionalised practices and culture that may perpetuate discrimination or exclusion, from recruitment and promotion processes to decision-making and ways of interacting with teams. *Challenging ourselves* requires the self-awareness and humility I talked of in previous chapters – honesty about our own limitations, and a willingness to hear criticism and learn from others.[14]

Inclusive leadership also requires commitment – the commitment and integrity to stay true to our values of fairness, inclusion and equity, even if that comes at personal risk. It requires commitment to follow-through on the decisions made by collaboration with our teams, commitment to hold meetings, invite contributions and lead our teams in ways that ensure all have a voice and feel connected, even if this takes more time or resource. Inclusive leadership requires commitment to prioritise inclusion in the workplace, and to clearly and compelling articulate the case for and the value of inclusion at work. Not only will this support the sense of belonging for members of our teams it will ultimately stimulate their engagement and motivation and their ability to add value and perform at their best for our organisations.

Notes

1 Bortini, P., Paci, A., Rise, A., & Rojnik, I. (2016). Inclusive leadership theoretical framework. *Creative Commons*, p. 19. Accessed at https://inclusiveleadership.eu/the-inclusive-leadership-handbook-theoretical-framework/
2 Dillon, B., & Bourke, J. (2016). *The six signature traits of inclusive leadership: Thriving in a diverse new world*. Westlake, Texas: Deloitte University Press.
3 Bortini, P., Paci, A., Rise, A., & Rojnik, I. (2016). Inclusive leadership theoretical framework. *Creative Commons*, p. 19. Accessed at https://inclusiveleadership.eu/the-inclusive-leadership-handbook-theoretical-framework/
4 Tapia, A. T., & Polonskaia, A. (2021). *The five disciplines of inclusive leadership: Unleashing the power of all of us*. San Francisco, CA: Berrett-Koehler Publishers.
5 Dillon, B., & Bourke, J. (2016). *The six signature traits of inclusive leadership: Thriving in a diverse new world*. Westlake, Texas: Deloitte University Press.
6 Dillon, B., & Bourke, J. (2016). *The six signature traits of inclusive leadership: Thriving in a diverse new world*. Westlake, Texas: Deloitte University Press.
7 Scharmer, O. (2009). *Theory U – Leading from the Future as It Emerges. The social technology of presencing*. San Francisco, CA: Berrett-Koehler Publishers, p. 384.
8 Martin, R. L. (2009). *The opposable mind: How successful leaders win through the art of integrative thinking*. Boston, MA: Harvard Business Press.

9 Olivier, S., Hölscher, F., & Williams, C. (2020). *Agile leadership for turbulent times: Integrating your ego, eco and intuitive intelligence.* London: Routledge.
10 Martin, R. L. (2009). *The opposable mind: How successful leaders win through the art of integrative thinking.* Boston, MA: Harvard Business Press.
11 Olivier, S., Hölscher, F., & Williams, C. (2020). *Agile leadership for turbulent times: Integrating your ego, eco and intuitive intelligence.* London: Routledge.
12 Liberating Structure developed by Henri Lipmanowicz and Keith McCandless.
13 Tapia, A. T., & Polonskaia, A. (2021). *The five disciplines of inclusive leadership: Unleashing the power of all of us.* San Francisco, CA: Berrett-Koehler Publishers.
14 Dillon, B., & Bourke, J. (2016). *The six signature traits of inclusive leadership: Thriving in a diverse new world.* Westlake, Texas: Deloitte University Press.

10
Reframing a sense of belonging

> I blame myself, in that, you know that's the other aspect of it for not belonging. It's because of something I've said or something I've done, or the way I've behaved or something. And you know, you end up having a real downer on yourself.
>
> – Neil, Head of Residential Care Home

The Ancient Greek Philosopher Epictetus once said: "Man is troubled, not by events, but by the meaning he gives to them."[1] The truth of this philosophy is reflected in the core of a sense of not belonging. The experience becomes significant to us, impacting our self-esteem and psychological well-being only when the *meaning* that we place on feeling that we do not belong has implications *who we are*. This too, distinguishes those for whom the experience is significant from those for whom it is not. Those individuals who experience a less significant, transient or situational sense of not belonging at work do not blame themselves for the experience, and as such whilst it may tell them something about how they behave, it says nothing about *who they are*. This is often either because they are in a position in which they have control over productively resolving their experience or most critically, they are able to appreciate that their experience is primarily a product of the situation – they are new in the company, they do not have the right skills or connections, there is a clear disparity between their values/aspirations/the job/organisation/opportunities. Therefore, the meaning of the experience bears no impact on their sense of self.

However, as addressed in Chapter 4, if we do not feel we have the control and resources to resolve the experience, or we squarely assign responsibility for the experience to ourselves, the sense of not belonging becomes a very negative and often recurring occurrence. In Chapters 5 and 6, I discussed the constructive and productive resolutions strategies that can help to lift us out of this experience. In this final chapter however, I would like to focus on meaning and sense-making – why attribution and the meaning we make of the experience

DOI: 10.4324/9781003108849-13

can impact us so negatively, and introduce some tools to help us more appropriately assign responsibility for a sense of not belonging in the workplace. Ultimately, this might help to prevent the spiral of not belonging, wrest us from this harmful experience and support the development of positive psychological well-being.

What sense of not belonging means for us

My most acute experience of not belonging occurred whilst working as a Business Development Manager. I had moved into the role in an attempt to move up in the organisation. I was in the middle of completing a master's degree in Occupational Psychology and thought that working with clients and faculty to help them understand the development that their leaders needed would be a valuable way to apply what I was learning. I thought it would be a perfect fit. In the reality of the situation, however, a number of factors conspired against me.

First, my role in the process of engaging with clients was unclear – whilst some faculty wanted my input into conversations with clients in terms of the background and broader services of the business school, others preferred me to take notes and support their inputs. They were the experts, not I. I therefore never really knew what value I added, what contribution I could make in those meetings. Second, only a week into the role I experienced a spectacular failure. I was asked to run a meeting with a very important potential client with a fairly inexperienced member of faculty. Neither of us really knew what we were talking about, did not know how to respond to the client's questions, and spent the entire hour 'deer in headlights.' That experience lay the foundations for my belief that I was not competent in the role. Third, the department itself was under a lot of pressure – we were the front line, the ones that were responsible for the income of the organisation – my bosses were stressed and stretched, and my line manager, in particular, had a clear idea of what we should be delivering, and the type of salesperson we needed to be to reach our targets. That person was not at all who I was. Lastly, about a year into the role I took maternity leave to have my first child. I returned after a year, working three days a week, still full of hormones and the guilt that so often accompanies working mums – not doing enough at home, not doing enough at work.

An objective, rational perspective on this scenario might determine that my sense of not belonging was down to (a) poor management – throwing me into a task I was clearly not ready for; (b) a lack of fit between what the role demanded and who I was/what I expected; (c) a lack of clarity on my value and contribution; and (d) a recognised phenomenon of guilt and self-flagellation experienced by working mothers. *Cause: the situation. Solution: change job.*

But that was not the story I told myself. My own personal, private narrative was that I was not good enough. I had nothing to add to the client meetings, no value to bring, was entirely lacking in the required competence to deliver this role and had taken a step way beyond my capabilities. I believed my boss thought they had made a huge mistake in hiring me and faculty did not want to work with me. I utterly blamed myself for the acute sense of not belonging I was experiencing, and as such did not share how I was feeling with anyone, stifling any potential development of relationships. *Cause: me. Solution: withdraw.*

You might perhaps be shaking your head in disbelief at my self-absorbed negative internal chatter. Or perhaps you are nodding quietly and reflectively to yourself as you recognise similar interpretations and sense-making you have applied to your own story-telling.

Whilst there is a stark difference between my interpretation and that of the outsider, this does not undermine either perspective – my subjective interpretation was my version of reality – it was what I experienced and felt, and therefore it was real. At its heart, the reason for these two contradictory realities are the attributions made about the experience and the underlying beliefs these communicate. The outsider attributes the cause of the experience to the situation whereas I attribute it to myself, resulting in the belief that I am not good enough, which in turn informs how I attempt to cope, my emotional experience, and shovels fuel onto the fire of my powerful inner critic.

Unconscious cognitions

As covered in Chapter 3, *Attribution Theory* argues and appraisal theories of emotion and research supports, attributing the cause of an event to ourselves – internal causality – will result in self-directed emotions.[2] Thus, holding ourselves accountable for a bad experience will lead to emotions such as guilt, frustration, anger or shame. According to *Self-Conscious Affect Theory*,[3] what then determines whether we feel guilt or shame is whether our interpretation results in a negative evaluation of our *behaviour* or a negative evaluation of the *self*. The former results in guilt and the latter in shame, and negative self-talk.

These different emotions, however, are also responsible for how we behave in response to the event. When we evaluate our behaviour negatively, we experience guilt, but whilst we attribute the cause to ourselves, we believe that behaviour to be unstable (something that can change), controllable (something *we* can change) and situation specific (something that is associated with a specific situation). As such, feelings of guilt encourage productive behaviours aimed at repairing the situation. When we evaluate *who we are* negatively however, we experience shame, and in this situation, whilst again attributing the cause to ourselves, we also believe the cause to be stable (something that cannot be changed), uncontrollable (something *we* cannot change), and global (something that is associated with all situations over time).[4] As such, rather than attempting to resolve the situation, we withdraw, we avoid, and we hide as explored in Chapter 4.[5, 6, 7] In so doing we create a vicious cycle – our feelings direct our focus to only that which supports our negative thoughts, overlooking alternative explanations and thus maintaining the negative perceptions we have created of ourselves.

Brené Brown, Research Professor at the University of Houston and prolific writer on courage, vulnerability and shame, proposes that in response to shame, we put up 'shame screens' – a defence mechanism designed to protect us and our sense of self. She argues that shame triggers our stress response of fight, flight or freeze, and as such in response to shame we either:

- *move against* shame by trying to gain control over others,
- *move away* from shame by withdrawing, staying silent and hiding how we are feeling or,
- *move towards* shame by seeking approval and a sense of belonging.[8]

All of these behaviours are evident in the accounts I have described in this book and the findings from research. Moving against shame manifests in some of the anti-social behaviours of excluded individuals such as becoming aggressive towards the individual we believe rejected us.[9] As discussed in Chapter 4, many who have experienced a sense of not belonging move away from shame by withdrawing and not disclosing experiences, whilst others move towards shame by seeking acceptance, approval and a way of behaving that they believe will render them acceptable. As such, our interpretation of not belonging not only serves to undermine our sense of self-esteem and self-worth, but the shame that is triggered by it and the lack of control we feel we have over it, also undermines our capacity to resolve the experience, leading to the poor coping choices and self-defeating behaviours, discussed in Chapter 4. This can become a painful, destructive spiral, and it is as such, essential that we become aware of these processes and can take steps towards breaking this chain.

So, how might we do that? There are lots of different methods to support the development of a positive self-concept, and it would be irresponsible of me to introduce many of them here as their effective and meaningful application requires professional intervention. As such, what I include here are some simple tools to raise awareness, encourage agency, development, and a shift in thinking.

Challenging our inner critic

We all have an inner critic, that negative internal voice that criticises our actions, our potential to achieve and at times our self-worth. Our negative internal monologue judges our decisions, actions and characteristics, blames us for negative events and mistakes and can threaten us with catastrophising statements. Inner critics can manifest as ubiquitous, perpetual negative self-perceptions as well as frequent automatic negative thoughts (ANTS) that arise without invitation in response to our experience. As I have discussed, they shape the way we interpret the world, they impact our decisions, undermine our sense of self and frequently inhibit productive behaviours, sabotaging any potential efforts to take positive action and disprove the thought.[10]

Table 10.1 is a typology of ANTS offered by PositivePsychology.com, some of which you may recognise in yourself:

Table 10.1 Typology of automatic negative thoughts

Type	Description	Example
Dichotomous "All-or nothing" Reasoning	Viewing things as either black or white, overlooking the possibility that things may lie on a spectrum	"He's either being entirely honest, or he's out to get me"
Arbitrary Inference	Drawing conclusions without all the facts	"He left the coffee lounge when I entered, I must have upset him"
Minimisation/ Magnification	Over-emphasising the negative situational attributes while playing down positive ones	"The presentation was a disaster because there was a typo in the heading"
Personalisation	Feeling personally to blame for things that are beyond your control	"It was my fault the client went with the competition"
Discounting the Positive	Identifying negatives in positive situations or events or turning positive results into negative ones	"She only said that because she wants a favour"

Reframing a sense of belonging

Type	Description	Example
Overgeneralisation	Drawing overly broad conclusions from standalone events; using singular cases to draw conclusions about all other events	"I was late because I'm bad at time management"
Global Judgements	Applying deprecatory or negative labels to standalone incidents or people	"Nobody values me"
Moral Imperatives	Applying a strict set of standards to everyone and everything, including oneself. Must, should, ought	"I must never be late"
Emotional Reasoning	Using one's feelings about something to rationalise one's thoughts	"I was anxious, therefore the meeting was badly run"
Selective Abstraction	Using a single or small negative attribute to draw conclusions regarding a whole scenario	"I mis-pronounced his name so the whole interview was a disaster"

Source: PositivePsychology.com[11]

One of the challenges to breaking the cycle of these negative thought patterns is their very nature. In the first instance, as they are automatic, they arise without us consciously processing them. They are also often habitual, so can become so normal, such an accepted part of our psyche that we take them for granted and pay them little attention. They are often also fleeting and rapid, and as such can pass through our minds too quickly for us to catch hold of and pay attention to them.[12] However, becoming aware of our own negative thoughts, when, where and why they occur is the first critical step in taming our inner critic, more constructively responding to the triggers of a sense of not belonging, and making more appropriate attributions for our experience.

Step one: awareness and acceptance

Awareness of negative thoughts and emotions is the key tenet of Brené Brown's *Shame Resilience Theory*.[13] The theory focuses on building resilience to shame by moving away from the fear, blame and disconnection associated with it, towards empathy, and courage, connection and compassion. This journey, Brown argues, requires four key steps:

1. *Recognising shame and understanding our triggers* – what situations, people, circumstances cause us to feel shame, and what physical responses do they stimulate, such as increased heart rate, flushing, constriction in our throat, that might help us to identify those triggers?

2. *Practising critical awareness* – understanding what has contributed to the construction of our shame response, such as our background, society, culture, and who and what benefits from our experience of shame.

3. *Reaching out and telling our story* – naming our experience, sharing our story, and obtaining support.

4. *Speaking shame* – moving away from silence and secrecy in order to diminish the power of shame.

As well as supporting development of our resilience to shame, developing awareness is also the first vital step in challenging our inner negative thoughts. Recognising the types of situation that give rise to them, listening for words that signal distorted thinking, such as 'must,' 'should,' 'ought,' 'can't,' 'never,' identifying physical responses such as butterflies, flushing or fidgeting, and spotting recurring themes will help us to detect and isolate them.[14] In the case of belonging, this means paying attention to the automatic thoughts that are triggered by any of those factors that contribute to a sense of not belonging: What do we tell ourselves if we are struggling to make connections at work, if we get over-looked in a conversation or a meeting? What does our inner critic tell us if we are anxious about a particular conversation with a difficult client, make a mistake in a presentation, fail to speak up in a meeting? What do we hear in our heads when we are working in a team who have different backgrounds, educations, ethnicities? What do we tell ourselves about our attempts to be accepted, about our tendency to withdraw, to conform, to defer? And what do our internal narratives tell us about what these feelings, facts, behaviours, this sense of not belonging, mean about who we are?

Curiosity and self-compassion

Deborah Lee, head of trauma services at Berkshire Healthcare, emphasises the importance of entering this enquiry with curiosity and self-compassion, which

Reframing a sense of belonging

she describes as "developing insight so that you can see yourself, rather than be yourself, as such. It's an ability to feel safe as opposed to traumatised – to develop the flexibility in your mind to develop a compassionate lens."[15] My coach that I referred to in Chapter 6 advised me too, that that which we resist will persist. If we attack our negative thoughts, try to push them away, confront them harshly, they will only gain strength. Rather, accepting that negative, distorted thoughts are a natural human experience, spotting them, exploring them with curiosity, openness and self-compassion allows us to take control of managing them and ultimately changing them.

Step two: challenge

The second critical step then is to challenge these thoughts. So often our automatic negative thoughts are at best exaggeratedly negative and at worst completely incorrect, and as discussed above, typically involve the incorrect or inappropriate attribution of blame and responsibility. As such, once we have identified these thoughts, these patterns of self-criticism, we need to explore them, understand on what they are based and investigate the evidence for the assumptions and conclusions we are making.

Dr Derek Lee, a Clinical Psychologist, identifies five steps to challenging and ultimately modifying our negative thoughts:

1 *Examining* – identifying the evidence both for and against the thought,
2 *Exploring* – the idiosyncratic meanings of the thought, what it represents and means to us,
3 *Exposing* – the inherent bias, distortion, assumptions upon which the thought is based,
4 *Expanding* – our perspective by considering alternative beliefs and propositions,
5 *Experimenting* – both behaviourally and cognitively, with different ways of thinking to develop a more balanced and constructive way of thinking.[16]

One approach to these steps is to begin with Socratic questioning, a type of questioning that explores the meaning, evidence and justification for assumptions that we make, thoughts we have, and viewpoints and perspectives we hold.[17] Below are some example Socratic questions designed for use by the individual to develop their own self-insight and examine many of the different types of automatic negative thoughts discussed above.[18]

- What is the evidence for this thought?
- Is this thought based on facts or feelings?
- Could I be misinterpreting the evidence? Am I making assumptions?
- Might other people have different interpretations of this same situation? What are they?
- Am I having this thought out of habit, or do the facts support it?
- Am I looking at all the evidence or just what supports my thought?
- Is my thought a likely scenario or the worst-case scenario?
- Besides myself, what else might be affecting this situation?
- Am I using "I must," "I have to," or "I should" thinking here? Is it truly necessary?

Through this interrogation we can start to unpick and undermine the thoughts and assumptions we are making that might be perpetuating or exacerbating our sense of not belonging.

So, let us put this into practice in Box 10.1, and begin with some of the questions above, considering some potential responses to those questions using an example from my research group. Sandra, who was Head of Finance in a public sector department described one of the times when she had felt like she did not belong was when she moved into a finance role leading a new team consisting of individuals who had a shared history, a shared language, more experience sometimes than she, and who had all worked in local government, whereas she had come from an accountancy background. This situation left her feeling that she did not belong, she did not fit in. It impacted her confidence to make decisions, to delegate work, to lead, to interact and establish relationships. She thought she did not belong.

Box 10.1

- What is the evidence for this thought? Sandra did not have good relationships with her team members as they did with each other and did not know as much as them about local government.

- Is this thought based on facts or feelings? Mainly feelings – understandable facts in terms of not having the same knowledge and relationships resulted in her feeling she did not fit in. She was

- guided by the anxiety and discomfort that she was feeling. The facts alone would not likely have dictated this thought.
- Could she be misinterpreting the evidence? Is she making assumptions? Yes, she interpreted the facts as evidence that she did not belong – did not fit in and was not accepted. And she was assuming that she was perceived by the team as an outsider.
- Might other people have different interpretations of this same situation? What are they? Others might interpret this as a challenging situation that will take time for her to establish her credibility, build relationships and trust, but that it would be a challenge for anyone in that situation. She is simply new.
- Is she looking at all the evidence or just what supports her thought? She told me that she later discovered that whilst her feelings were stopping her from making decisions and delegating, that her team were looking to her for that. So, it would seem she over-looked evidence that she was in fact, being accepted.
- Is she having this thought out of habit, or do the facts support it? The facts do not support it, but the experience was one of many, and as such, assuming she does not fit in when she is new to a team or role is likely a habit.

Step three: reframe

The final step to challenging our negative thoughts and attributions is to reframe them, to create an alternative appraisal of the situation that stimulated the thought. This is not of course a straightforward and simple process. What we think, what we believe, not only informs our self-concept, but is informed *by* it – so having a negative self-concept will ultimately encourage negative thoughts and beliefs. As I mentioned at the start of this section, there are many different approaches to developing positive psychological well-being many of which focus on the lower level of the iceberg – our identity, but it would be irresponsible of me to encourage you to practice with those independently here. But if we can start to shift our *thinking*, tap small chinks in the armour of our inner critic we can start down the road of self-confidence that will provide us with the foundations to make bolder strides. The aim here is not to silence or switch off our inner critic, but to develop an alternative, positive narrative to counter it.

Drawing on the evidence we have gathered through our exploration and questioning we need to capture an alternative thought, an alternative way of interpreting the situation that triggered our negative thinking. Given this situation what would we say to a friend or loved one, what alternative belief or interpretation might we offer to them? What words would we use and what tone would we use? We need then to use these words and tone with ourselves.

Thought records are a simple but effective way of capturing this process of cognitive reframing and can help us to break the cycle by impacting how we behave. Box 10.2 includes such a thought record along with an example of how reframing can be applied.

Box 10.2 Example positive belief record

Belief	Alternate belief
I messed up the meeting because I'm incompetent	I messed up because I didn't have any experience
Evidence	**Evidence**
The meeting went terribly, and we didn't win the business	I had been in the job for 5 days
	I had had no development
Emotion	**Emotion**
Shame	Frustration
Action	**Action**
Withdrawal and disengagement	Prepare, ask, seek support

Source: Positivepsychology.com[19]

This process takes practice. But the more often we practice – becoming aware of our negative thoughts, what they sound like, when they arise; exploring with self-compassion their validity, their truth; and then identifying an alternative, more positive thought – the better we will become at appropriately interpreting our experience of not belonging, diverting the focus of our response to our behaviour rather than what is says about who we are, and establishing a sense of agency in our experience which will both support our psychological well-being and our sense of belonging.

Notes

1 Das, L. S. (2007). *The big questions: How to find your own answers to life's essential mysteries*. Emmaus, PA: Rodale Books, p. 39.
2 Weiner, B. (1985). An attributional theory of achievement motivation and emotion. *Psychological Review*, 92(4), 548–573. https://doi:10.1037//0033-295x.92.4.548
3 Lewis, H. B. (1971). *Shame and guilt in neurosis*. New York: Intentional University Press.
4 Lewis, H. B. (1971). *Shame and guilt in neurosis*. New York: Intentional University Press.
5 Tangney, J. P. (1993). Shame and guilt. In C. G. Costello (Ed.) *Symptoms of depression*. Oxford: John Wiley & Sons, 161–180.
6 Niedenthal, P. M., Tangney, J. P., & Gavanski, I. (1994). 'If only I weren't' versus 'If only I hadn't': distinguishing shame and guilt in counterfactual thinking. *Journal of Personality and Social Psychology*, 67, 585–595. https://doi.org/10.1037/0022-3514.67.4.585
7 Tracy, J. L., & Robins, R. W. (2006). Appraisal antecedents of shame and guilt: Support for a theoretical model. *Personality and Social Psychology Bulletin*, 32, 1339–1351. https://doi.org/10.1177/0146167206290212
8 Brown, B. (2008). I thought it was just me (but it isn't): Telling the truth about perfectionism. New York: Gotham Books.
9 Gerber, J. P., & Wheeler, L. (2009a). On being rejected: A meta-analysis of experimental research on rejection. *Perspectives on Psychological Science*, 4, 468–488. https://doi:10.1111/j.1745-6924.2009.01158.x
10 Potter, A. (1998). *Putting the positive thinker to work*. New York: Berkley Books.
11 Typology of automatic negative thoughts. Source: Positive.Psychology.com
12 Beck, A. T. (1987). Cognitive models of depression. *Journal of Cognitive Psychotherapy: An International Quarterly*, 1, 5–37.
13 Brown, B. (2008). I thought it was just me (but it isn't): Telling the truth about perfectionism. New York: Gotham Books.
14 Beck, A. T. (1987). Cognitive models of depression. *Journal of Cognitive Psychotherapy: An International Quarterly*, 1, 5–37.
15 Hunt. E. (2021). Silence your inner critic: A guide to self-compassion in the toughest times. *The Guardian*, January 2021.
16 Dr Derek Lee. Downloaded from https://psychodelights.com/pdfs/cbt_nats.pdf
17 Brookfield, S. D. (2011). *Teaching for critical thinking: Tools and techniques to help students question their assumptions*. San Francisco, CA: Jossey-Bass.
18 Clark, G. I., & Egan, S. J. (2015). The Socratic method in cognitive behavioural therapy: A narrative review. *Cognitive Therapy and Research*, 39(6), 863–879. https://doi.org/10.1007/s10608-015-9707-3
19 Positive belief record. Source: Positive.psychology.com

Conclusion

The journey of belonging

When I first began my research into a sense of not belonging back in 2012 it was a fairly undiscussed and under-researched phenomenon, particularly in the context of the workplace. Whilst the word resonated for those who had experienced an absence of belonging, it meant little to those who had not. But since that time the management arena has borne witness to a notable shift of focus in our organisations, from one keenly observing performance, output and results, to one that pays more attention to people – to their experience in the workplace – their well-being, their resilience, their work-home balance, their engagement, their sense of purpose and their sense of belonging.

With this welcome shift has been a move towards a more humble approach to leadership, to the appreciation of the characteristics of compassion, humility, the courage to be vulnerable and the acceptance of psychological challenges that go hand in hand with leadership and say nothing about an individual's capacity to lead. My hope is that my openness and candour in the sharing of my own experiences in this book offers an encouraging example of the value of that humility.

These changes have occurred gradually over the past decade. But what has changed more rapidly is a magnified focus on the importance of inclusion and belonging which has erupted over the past 12 months of writing this book following the outrage and the shift in public opinion that came in the aftermath of the murder of George Floyd in May 2020. This has shone a shining, uncomfortable but necessary light on the diversity of our workforces, the equity of our policies and practices, the inclusivity of our leadership and the sense of belonging of our employees. Inclusion and belonging have now made their way into the common vernacular. When I revisit Google with a search for the term 'sense of belonging' I am now alerted to 'about' 245,000,000 hits. Nearly 100 million more than eight months ago.

DOI: 10.4324/9781003108849-14

Interest and understanding are growing in the importance and impact of a sense of belonging at work, both for our well-being and for our performance. And leaders are recognising their role and their ability to support that for their teams. It is my hope that this book supports them in that journey.

Maya Angelou, poet, author, civil rights activist, speaker and dancer once said: "I long, as does every human being, to be at home wherever I find myself".[1] My hope too is that a serendipitous outcome of this shift in consciousness is the awareness for those who have or are still experiencing a sense of not belonging at work of the prevalence of this experience. Through this awareness, I hope they come to realise that they are not alone, and in so doing will feel less like an outsider, less that they do not belong and more able to be at home wherever they find themselves.

Note

1 Quoted in. Braun, A. M. (2019). Psychological inclusion: Considering students' feelings of belongingness and the benefits for academic achievement. In M. J. Schuelka, C. J. Johnstone, G. T. Alfredo, & J. Artiles (Eds.) *The SAGE handbook on inclusive and diversity in education*, 66–75, p. 66. http://dx.doi.org/10.4135/9781526470430.n8

Index

Note: Locators in *italics* refer to figures and those in **bold** to tables.

abilities *see* strengths
active listening 70–72
adaptive nature of belonging 15–16, 49
adding value: developing strengths 85–88; identifying strengths 78–82; importance of 26–27, 78; leveraging strengths 83–84; perceived differences 29; performance and belonging 48–49
affinity bias 96
ageism bias 97
agency 54
Alderfer, C. P. 10–11
Angelou, Maya 137
anterior cingulate cortex (ACC) 17
anxiety 44
arbitrary inference **128**
Ascent to Competence Conceptual Framework 38–39
attentive listening 71–72
attribution theory 44–45, 126
authenticity 49–52, 74–75, 109
automatic negative thoughts (ANTS) **128–129**, 128–134
autonomy 4, **119**

banter 24, 33, 51–53
Baumeister, Roy 11–12
being human 75–77
being ourselves 49–52, 74–76
belonging hypothesis 11–12
belonging, sense of: factors undermining 22–30, 125–126; organisational culture 3, 31–33; reframing 5, 124–134; in the workplace 2–3, 22, 136–137

bias: continued existence of 4–5, 92–94; expectations 29; self-awareness 101–102; types of 96–97; unconscious 95–97, 102
black, indigenous, and people of colour (BIPOC): addressing discrimination 100–103; continuation of racial inequity 94–100; continued existence of prejudice, discrimination and bias 92–94; forms of diversity 91–92; perceived differences 28, 29, 90
Black Lives Matter 29, 90, 93–94
body language 71, 72–73, 74
BOFF feedback model 85–86, *86*
Brown, Brené 130
bystander apathy 14–15

caring for others 111–112
Clance, Pauline 42
cliques 13, 15–16, 23–24
coaching 86–87; *see also* mentoring programs
cognitive crafting 84
cognitive dissonance 51
collaboration 117–120
colonial history 94
colour-blindness 98–99
compassion for others 111–112
compassion for self 130–131
compassionate discomfort 102
confidence 38–39
confirmation bias 96
conformity theory 43–44, 50–51
connectivity 25
contrast effect 97
control: *vs.* autonomy **119**; need for 53–56
conversations: active listening 70–72; inclusive leaders 120–121; interpersonal skills 110–111; knowing others 68–74

coping strategies 55–56, **55–56**
courage 121–122
Covey, Stephen 70, *71*
cultural intelligence 117; *see also* diversity
culture *see* organisational culture
curiosity 130–131

Deci, E. L. 11
depression 44
DiAngelo, Robin 99–100
dichotomous reasoning **128**
differences, and belonging 28–30, 90; *see also* diversity
discrimination: addressing 100–103; continuation of racial inequity 94–100; continued existence of 4–5, 92–94; inclusive leaders 121–122
diversity 4–5, 90–91; addressing discrimination 100–103; continuation of racial inequity 94–100; continued existence of prejudice, discrimination and bias 92–94; forms of 91–92; inclusive leaders 115
diversity and inclusion (D&I) training 92

Edmondson, Amy 108, 110
emotional carrying capacity 25
emotional experience 25
emotional reasoning **129**
emotions: in conversations 70; self-blame 44–45; unconscious cognitions 126–128
empathetic listening 70, 72
empathy 13, 107, 110
ethnocentrism 12
evolutionary psychology 15–16
existence, relatedness and growth needs (ERG) 10–11
expectations 29; *see also* social norms

failure, tolerance of 112
feedback 85–86, *86*
fight-flight-freeze response 16–17
Fisher, Eileen 110
Floyd, George 90, 94, 99

gender bias 96
global judgements **129**
Goleman, Daniel 87

group structures: differences 28–29; establishing relationships 64–66; human need for belonging 12, 13; psychological safety 107–108
groupthink 13–14
GROW model 87–88
growth needs 10–11

Hagerty, B. M. K. 27
harassment, racial 92
Hewlin, Patricia 44, 50–51
hierarchy of needs 10, *11*, 39
homosexuality, bias against 97
hormones 17
horn and halo affect 96–97
Howard, John 12
human behaviour: adaptive nature of belonging 15–16; human need for belonging 12–13; motivators 10–11, 57–58; neuroscience of belonging 16–18; social norms 15
human need for belonging 3, 9–18; adaptive nature of belonging 15–16; motivators of behaviour 10–11; neuroscience 16–18; universality 11–15
humility 109–110, 116–117

Imes, Suzanne 42
imposter syndrome 42
inauthenticity 51
inclusion, and diversity 91, 92, 93–94
inclusive leaders 5; behaviours 117–121; courage and commitment 121–122; how to be 115–116; mindsets 116–117; psychological safety 114
Inclusive Leadership Approach (ILA) 115
Inner critic **128–129**, 128–134
institutional racism 95
integrative thinking 118–119
intelligence, diversity 100–101, 117
interdependency 64
interpersonal skills 110–111

job-crafting 83–84

knowing others 66–74
knowing yourself 74–76, 79–82; *see also* self-concept

Index

Lathlean, Judith 38–39
Lawrence, Stephen 95
leadership: promoting a sense of belonging 2–3, 4–5; psychological safety 109–114; trust 73–74; *see also* inclusive leaders
Leary, Mark 11–12, 40
Lee, Derek 131
Levett-Jones, Tracy 38–39
listening skills 70–72, 73–74

Martin, Roger 118
Maslow, Abraham 10, *11*, 39
McClelland, D. C. 11
meaningful relationships 66–77; *see also* relationships at work
Mehrabian, Albert 73
mentoring programs 64; *see also* coaching
micro-aggressions 97–98
micro-inequities 98
micro-interventions 102–103
mindsets 116–117
minorities: addressing discrimination 100–103; continuation of racial inequity 94–100; continued existence of prejudice, discrimination and bias 92–94; forms of diversity 91–92; perceived differences 28, 29, 90
mood 44–45
moral imperatives **129**
motivators, human behaviour 10–11, 57–58
Mueller, Jennifer 99

need for belonging *see* human need for belonging
negative thoughts **128–129**, 128–134
neuroscience of belonging 16–18

openness 76, 110, 116, 117
ordinary hero, the 72
organisational culture 3, 31–33; inability to change 54–55; psychological safety 106, 107, 112–114
overgeneralisation **129**
oxytocin 17

perceptions: establishing relationships 64–66; forms of diversity 91–92; knowing others 66–74; knowing yourself 74–76; perceived differences 28–30, 90
performance, and belonging 4, 48–58; ability to be ourselves 49–52; need for control 53–56; perceived differences 29; self-protection 52–53
performance reviews 79, 83, 85–86
permission to care 111–112
personal strengths: developing 85–88; identifying 78–82; leveraging 83–84; *see also* adding value
personal values assessment 82
Porter, Elias Hull 66–67
positive beliefs **134**
prefrontal cortex 17–18
prejudice: continued existence of 92–94; self-awareness 101–102; as self-defence mechanism 13
psychological safety 5, 106; definition 106–109; fostering 109–113; inclusive conversations 120–121; inclusive leaders 114; organisational culture 32–33
psychometric tools 66–67

quality relationships 66–77; *see also* relationships at work

racism: addressing discrimination 100–103; continuation of racial inequity 94–100; continued existence of prejudice, discrimination and bias 4–5, 92–94; fear of stepping in 100; ignorance 98–100; micro-aggressions 97–98; micro-inequities 98; perceived differences 29, 90; as self-defence mechanism 13; structural and systemic 94–95, 102; unconscious bias 95–97, 102
recruitment 92, 97
relatedness needs 10–11
relationship crafting 84
relationships at work 4; as challenge 63; establishing relationships 63–66; importance of 23–26, 63; meaningfulness 66–77
remote working 64–65
right ventral prefrontal cortex (RVPFC) 17–18
Robbers Cave experiments 12
Rothbart, Myron 12
Ryan, R. M. 11

Index

safety, sense of *see* psychological safety
Schein, Edgar 31
Scudder, Tim 67
selective abstraction **129**
selective listening 71
self-awareness 79–80, 101–102, 116–117, 130
self-belief 38–39
self-blame 44–45
self-compassion 130–131
self-concept 3–4; being ourselves 49–52, 74–76; challenging our inner critic **128–129**, 128–134; coherent sense of 42–44; conformity theory 51; definition 37; mood and emotion 44–45; well-being 37–44; *see also* knowing yourself
self-conflict 42–43
Self-Conscious Affect Theory 126
self-defence strategies 13, 53–54
self-determination theory 11
self-efficacy 29–30, 38–39, 87–88
self-esteem 39–42, 52
self-protection 52–53
sense of fit 27, 31, 51
Shame Resilience Theory 130
Sharmer, Otto 117–118
Sherif, Muzafer 12
skills: developing strengths 85–88; identifying strengths 78–82; leveraging strengths 83–84; listening 70–72, 73–74
social bonds 12, 17; *see also* relationships at work
social identity theory 12
social monitoring 49–50
social norms: bystander apathy 14–15; conformity 50–52; groupthink 13–14
sociometer hypothesis 40
Socratic questioning 131–132
Space Shuttle Challenger disaster 14
status 29–30
stereotypes 96, 97–98, 101–102, 116; *see also* bias

'stinky fish' *113*
Strength Deployment Inventory 66–67, 79
strengths: developing 85–88; identifying 78–82; leveraging 83–84; *see also* adding value
structural racism 94–95, 102
survival, fight-flight-freeze response 16–17
systemic racism 94–95, 102

task crafting 84
teams 4; establishing relationships 64–66; human need for belonging 12, 13; perceived differences 28–29; psychological safety 107–108
tensility 25
threats, responding to 16–17
3-needs theory 11
trust 72–74, 107

unconscious bias 95–97, 102
universality of need to belong 11–15; *see also* human need for belonging

value *see* adding value
valued involvement 27
values: meaning, pleasure and strengths 81–82; organisational culture 31–32; permission to care 111–112; personal values assessment 82
virtual environments 64–65
vulnerabilities 75–77, 109–110, 116–117

well-being: and belonging 3–4, 36–37, 44–45; mood and emotion 44–45; self-concept 37–44
white fragility 99–100
white privilege 94–95, 101–102
Whitmore, John 87

yourself *see* knowing yourself; self-concept

Printed in the United States
by Baker & Taylor Publisher Services